CHANGING TIMES

Quality for Humans in a Digital Age

Rich Rogers

HEDDON PUBLISHING

www.heddonpublishing.com
www.facebook.com/heddonpublishing
@PublishHeddon

Foreword

The late great quality thinker Dr Edwards Deming once famously said that "quality is everyone's responsibility". In the context of his writings and working career, the 'everyone' referred to the people inside of the organisations who adopted his methods. Dr Deming passed away in 1993, which was one year before IBM released the IBM Simon, the world's first smartphone, and about two years before the internet exploded into the mainstream. I'm sure Dr Deming could never have envisaged how pervasive technology products would become in our everyday lives. Perhaps if he'd lived for another 25 years he might have added to his "quality is everyone's responsibility" statement, something along the lines of "because everyone is impacted by technology quality". Today, everyone, from two-year-olds to ninety-two-year-olds, seems to be more and more dependent on technology products.

To understand how dependent we've all become, just think about how productive you were the last time your office systems or connection to the internet went down for even a few hours. On a personal level, think about how weird it felt the last time you arrived at work in the morning to discover that you'd accidentally left your smartphone at home. If you're like me, you'd be compelled to go home again and get it; I feel so disconnected without it. Our relationship with technology is more intertwined than ever and the human-to-machine relationship is not a simple one.

This is why we're all impacted by the quality of technology, whether we like it or not.

In today's digital world, most people using technology products rarely stop to think about how the quality of those products impacts their lives. But it does. Sometimes in very subtle, almost invisible, ways, and other times in incredibly annoying, frustrating, pull-your-hair-out ways.

So, if we're all impacted by technology quality, who are the people responsible for creating the quality products we're using? How do they build quality into these products? How do they ensure that the customers' needs are met? If you've ever pondered on these and other questions about software and technology quality, this is a book for you.

Many books have been written about technology quality over the years and I have read a lot of them. The majority of these books tend to focus on teaching the reader the methods, processes and tools for practitioners to adopt within their working day. As useful as these books are for the 'insiders', they are not very accessible for mere mortal readers outside of the quality industry. It would also be a stretch to ever describe these types of books as engaging or page-turners. What Rich has done in this book is to recognise that the gap between people in technology and everyday business and their customers is wide. To bridge this gap, Rich has cleverly created an engaging story that everyone can relate to. A story that weaves the subtle and not-so-subtle impact technology has on us, as we go about our daily routine. By making technology challenges real to us in an everyday context, we can all get to a shared understanding of the quality concepts discussed, regardless of our level of expertise. This is a real skill and immediately opens up the book to a broad range of potential readers. If you are in business, information technology or merely an everyday consumer of technology products, this book will help you better understand the wonderful and sometimes confusing world of technology quality.

Tony Bailey
Human Quality Creator and Chief Executive Officer AccessHQ,
Sydney 2017

Preface

When I told people that I was writing a book, quite naturally the first thing they usually asked was:

"What's it about?"

I found that I needed different answers for this - depending on how interested they were: a short sentence (for people who were just being polite), and a slightly longer answer (for people who were genuinely interested, or perhaps unable to think of a good way to get out of the conversation).

Since you are reading this, I will assume that you have a genuine interest in the book and would therefore prefer the full answer: This is a book about quality; specifically, quality in software and technology. In part, this is an exploration of the rather nebulous concept of quality and some of the ways that we, as humans, perceive it. The examples typically relate to the sort of technology we use in our everyday lives – websites, applications and devices, which so many of us depend on in so much of what we do.

It is also a book about people: those who use technology, and the feelings they can experience as a result, but also the people who create and maintain that technology, and some of the challenges they face. For this reason, it is also a book about processes; the actions and methods associated with how technology is developed.

As we explore some of the examples in the book, we will also see the effect that technology has had, and continues to have, on many aspects of our lives in these changing times.

In case you're wondering, the shorter answer to the question is: This is a book about people and our relationship with technology.

The theme of quality as a 'relationship' between people and technology is not a new one. It is mentioned in blog posts by the creators of the 'Rapid Software Testing' methodology; James Bach in *The Quality Creation Myth* and Michael Bolton in a post outlining *The Premises of Rapid Software Testing*. This line from Michael's blog post stuck in my mind:

"Product quality is a relationship between a product and people, never an attribute that can be isolated from a human context."

The more time I have spent considering this subject, the more I have concluded that it helps to think about quality in this way. Most people understand relationships. We understand what we value in relationships, what matters to us, and what matters rather less. We know what fills us with joy and what annoys or irritates us. We recognise those traits which endear others to us, and those which frustrate us. We can identify what puts us at ease and what puts us on edge.

Our relationship with technology is not so different. We may not always pay as much attention to the feelings and emotional responses generated through our interactions with technology but those responses are there. We form relationships with technology, some of which are rewarding and lasting and others which are short-lived and can be fulfilling or wholly unsatisfying.

I will explore these themes in this book and look at some of the ways we decide whether the relationships are positive and productive or, perhaps, unhelpful and frustrating.

My interest in this subject goes back many years; certainly for the duration of my working life; prior to that as a student of business and technology, and probably even during my formative years. I can recall being fascinated by VHS machines, digital watches and calculators. Perhaps tellingly, I was less interested in the internal workings, the circuit boards, wires and chips, and more in the way these gadgets were designed and how they could help us in day-to-day life.

Since the mid-1990s I have worked in the development of software and technology products. For almost all of that time I have been involved in testing such products. I feel grateful for this because I believe testing presents a fantastic opportunity to represent the interests of the people who will use the products we work on; to consider those products from their point of view and to identify ways we might make their relationship with technology more positive.

Working with different organisations, of varying sizes and with diverse purposes, has given me the opportunity to observe the way people work in product development and support. It can be chaotic, and sometimes the results are less than impressive. Unfortunately, it isn't unusual for quality to be forgotten when projects are not going well (and sometimes even when things *are* going well). Regardless of this, the work which goes on, the enthusiasm for ideas, and the dedication to making those ideas real, can be inspiring.

A second question which I have been asked about the book is:

"Who is it for?"

Perhaps the best way to address this is to explain something of the purpose of the book. Firstly, it is intended to help those of us who work on technology products to think about quality from a human perspective (most of us are human too). Because of the field we work in, we can sometimes get caught up in the technical nature of our work, perhaps forgetting that the technology we create is ultimately intended to benefit people. We can lose sight of the humans at the centre of what we do. The stories and ideas in the book are designed to help us better understand what quality means to the people who use our products.

Secondly, the book may provide an insight for people who haven't worked in software or technology development into some of the things we do (or don't do), which might affect the way technology works (or doesn't work) for them. We will also explore some of the reactions and feelings which we can all experience when using technology, and some of the different factors which can cause them.

I hope, therefore, that the book will appeal to the many people around the world who design, develop, support and maintain software and other technology. I believe there are also valuable messages for the people who run, and define the purpose of, the organisations that provide their customers with technology; whether in the form of devices and software, or services supported by websites, apps, and so on.

I don't, however, want to limit the book's audience to technical people and, with that in mind, there may be places where I briefly explain concepts involved in developing software or technology. To people familiar with those concepts or ways of working, the explanations may seem somewhat simplified, or light on detail, but I make no apology for this. There are many detailed and specialised books available. This one is also about, and for, humans, irrespective of their technical knowledge.

There is one more question about the book which I should address here:

"How is it structured?"

To help you to get the most from the content, it might help if I explain the way the book is organised. Firstly, you should know that there is a story which flows through the book. The story concerns a journalist called Kim, and some of the ways in which technology affects her life. Kim's story is divided into chapters. Following each of these chapters are sections exploring themes related to quality and technology. These are loosely coupled with the story, taking examples from Kim's experiences (along with other examples) to explore the subject.

The book includes a model called 'Three Dimensions of Quality', which is intended to show three important factors which can affect the impression people form of the products they use. The three dimensions - Desirable, Dependable and Durable - are explored in dedicated sections where we will also look at some related aspects of quality.

Following this Preface, there is an explanation of some of the words and phrases which are used in the book. These will help to define some of the terms which are frequently used, and some others which may crop up less frequently but which might not be familiar to all readers.

Finally, at the end of the book, there are references and suggestions for further reading, including links to books, articles and websites.

I hope you enjoy reading *Changing Times* as much as I have enjoyed researching and writing it.

Rich Rogers,
Sydney, 2017
www.richrtesting.com
@richrtesting

Words and terms

To help readers who may not be familiar with all of the words and terms in the book, especially those associated with the development of software and other technology work, I have provided a brief explanation of some of them below.

The following definitions only relate to the use of the words and terms in the context of this book, and may differ from definitions elsewhere, or other people's views on what they should mean.

Key words

Customer - someone who uses a product, sometimes (but not always) following a financial payment which allows them to do so. Payments might be made as a single direct transaction, a subscription, or indirectly: through taxes, or banking fees, for example. Customers may 'pay' for a product through other indirect means, for example by providing companies with data, or by increasing advertising revenue by visiting a website.

Empathy - an ability to understand how another person might feel in a given set of circumstances, or to be able to experience something from their perspective; to 'put yourself in the shoes of another person'.

Product - a physical object (such as a phone or computer) or an application, website or computer system. Products could include packaging and accessories, and also software updates and support mechanisms, all of which might be included in the price a customer pays, and all of which could contribute to the impression they form of the product.

Purpose - the reason for doing something or, in the case of a product, the reason for its existence.

Quality - there are many definitions of Quality. The one which best serves the purpose of this book is Gerald Weinberg's definition: "Quality is value to some person". The words *value*, *valued* and *valuable* occur in the text when discussing the quality of products, as will references to the *relationship* between humans and technology (as discussed in the Preface). I will also talk about quality as a subjective and variable *impression* of a product or service.

Technology - the devices, applications, systems and other products developed through the application of technical knowledge and engineering skills. Typically, in this book, the term refers to digital or computer technology.

Business

Customer Experience – a term commonly used in businesses and other organisations to describe the totality of a customer's interaction with that organisation. This is certainly not limited to their experiences with technology products, but as technology becomes more deeply woven into the services provided by many organisations, it will play a more significant role in the customer experience.

Digital Revolution – the era of change which has seen much of human life become supported or assisted by digital technology. The Digital Revolution has seen the rise of computers, portable devices such as tablets and smartphones, and, crucially, the internet, which has fundamentally altered many aspects of our lives.

Early adopters – those people who are among the first to try a product or service, sometimes paying a premium for the privilege.

Retargeting – a marketing technique used to track a potential customer's interest in companies or their products, based on website visits. Adverts relating to those companies and products are displayed on other websites which the potential customer subsequently visits.

Time to market – the time it takes to develop a product, from conception to being made available to customers.

Touch points – moments of interaction between customers and organisations, however these interactions occur. Touch points significantly influence the impression a customer forms of an organisation.

Development of Software and Technology

App – a shortened version of 'application', meaning a software program. The word 'app' is often used when referring to an application which is installed and operated on a mobile device such as a smartphone or tablet.

Defect – a word used in some development teams to identify a fault or flaw in an application or system. Typically, this term is used to indicate a deviation from some documented requirement or predicted behaviour.

Exit Criteria – a list used in some software development projects to identify a point at which the process can move from one phase or stage into another. Essentially, this list describes a desired state, intended to represent a point at which it is believed to be acceptable to proceed from the completion of one activity to the start of some other activity.

Persona – a fictional person intended to represent real potential customers. Personas are used during product development as a way of keeping people's needs in mind during design and testing of products.

Quality Characteristics or Quality Criteria – a set of factors which are believed to affect the perceived quality of a product or service.

Release – this word can be used to describe the process or action of delivering a product to customers (e.g. "We will release at the end of the month."), or to identify a specific version or build of an application or system (e.g. "There's a problem with Release 6.3.1.").

Requirements – a pre-defined and often documented list of features and behaviours intended to capture what someone using a product might want or need from it.

Test Case – commonly used in software testing, a test case is a pre-scripted set of steps which describe some actions to be taken and an anticipated outcome based on those actions. The steps and outcomes are guided by how the software requirements are interpreted by the person who creates the test case.

Techniques, Practices and Methodologies

A/B Testing – a technique used to compare two versions of a product (a website or application, for example). The different versions, which may only vary slightly from each other, are made available to customers, whose responses and actions are tracked against each version. Their behaviour can provide companies with valuable insight into how the versions of the product compare and which is more likely to meet their customers' needs and their business goals.

Agile – a term which is used to capture a range of methods and practices, and a culture, influenced by the principles of the *Manifesto for Agile Software Development*. Agile development is intended to enable teams and organisations to react rapidly to changes in market conditions and customer demands through effective communication and close collaboration between people with business and technical knowledge.

Continuous Deployment – an approach for frequent release of software to customers. Continuous Deployment relies heavily on automation of many of the activities involved in software development, and on automation of the mechanisms by which software is released (deployed).

Lean – a set of principles and practices inspired by Japanese manufacturing methods, notably those employed by Toyota. Lean approaches emphasise reduction of waste, continuous improvement of processes, and delivery of value to customers.

Minimum viable product (MVP) – a basic, initial version of a product with enough features to release it to customers, from whom it can be learned how the product can be enhanced and cultivated.

Product Owner – a key role in the Scrum Framework (see below), a Product Owner is the person responsible for understanding the needs and wishes of customers and business stakeholders, and for articulating these to the people involved in developing the product.

Scrum Framework – a software development framework aligned with Agile principles. Development teams work in pre-defined time periods called 'sprints' to deliver elements of a product from a prioritised list called a 'backlog'. At the end of a sprint, work begins on the next elements from the list. The approach to product development is therefore incremental.

User stories – succinct descriptions of a feature (or requirement) of a product, expressed from the point of view of someone who will use that product.

V-model – an extension to the Waterfall model (see below), which aligns the Waterfall phases with 'verification and validation' activities intended to confirm the correctness of outputs. As with the Waterfall model, activities are carried out sequentially, with dependencies between the phases.

Waterfall – a software development model which is based on moving through phases of activity sequentially. The output (for example, requirements documents, or code) from one phase is required in order to carry out the next, and these dependencies discourage change and rework.

Miscellaneous

Capacity planning – in the context of computer systems, capacity planning refers to the management of the technical resources (memory, storage, processing power, etc.) required to enable those systems to cope with demand. This can include monitoring of system use, tuning of systems, and scaling capacity up and down as required.

Cloud storage – a method of storage which allows people or companies to store their data on remote (rather than attached or local) server computers. Typically, a company will provide cloud storage through a subscription service which allows customers to lease storage capacity.

Cognitive bias – an error in thinking which influences our decisions and judgements. A cognitive bias can result from experiences, memories, and our perceptions of reality.

Denial of service attacks – a deliberate attempt to disrupt or disable a computer system or network by overloading it. This is a kind of malicious cyber-attack intended to prevent people who need to use those systems or networks from doing so.

Empathy gap – A gap between what one person believes another person might feel in certain circumstances - or how they might respond - and how that other person actually feels and responds; an inability to empathise with another person.

Hosted applications – applications which people can use on their own computers but which are installed on remote computers and made available over the internet. Hosted software is sometimes provided on a subscription basis and referred to as Software as a Service (SaaS).

Human-Centered Design – an approach to problem solving which focuses on the needs and desires of people, involves them in the stages of the design process, and is intended to result in solutions (or products) which meet those needs and desires.

Urban Design – the methods and processes associated with designing urban areas, including housing and residential development, commercial areas and public spaces. Urban design is concerned with the relationship between people and the places they occupy.

Chapter One: Up and out

A gentle melody crept into Kim's consciousness. As she emerged from the comfort of a deep sleep, she groaned, wishing for silence once more. She reached out to her bedside table, searching for the source of the sound: her phone and the alarm which she had set the previous evening. She refused to open her eyes, clinging instead to the pleasant haziness which greeted the start of the new day.

The last remnants of peace were shattered as she knocked a book onto the floor, where it landed with a thud. Kim cursed and sat up. She located her phone and swiped the screen to silence the tune. Blinking as she adjusted to the daylight, she instinctively proceeded to unlock the device, pressing her index finger onto the button below the screen.

As was often the case, the day started with a scroll through the feed on her favourite social media app. The app was open – a reminder that this was also how she often ended the day. She knew it wasn't healthy to look at her phone just before sleeping - that she wasn't really allowing her brain to wind down at the end of the day - but the constant availability of information, news, opinions and arguments was addictive.

Kim Harris was a name known to sport-lovers in Australia due to her articles for the *Sydney Times*, the newspaper where she worked. She had amassed an army of followers through her various social media accounts. They were mainly people who were interested in reading the articles and links she shared but some wanted to engage with her directly, either to praise her for articles she had written herself, or to challenge what they had read in those articles. Sometimes these challenges could get out of hand. Like many other female journalists, Kim experienced 'trolling' and online bullying and this had led her to avoid direct discussions with people she didn't know. In particular, there seemed to be a vociferous group who struggled to accept that a female sports writer would comment on their male sporting heroes. Sadly, 'block' and 'report' features had become increasingly familiar to her.

Amongst the updates in her feed that morning was a link which someone had posted to a story about poor circulation figures for the *Times*. She followed the link, which took her to a page on a rival paper's website. A huge car advertisement obscured much of the content and as Kim tried to scroll down to read the story, she inadvertently touched the advert. Immediately, she was redirected to another browser window, this time featuring the website of the car company. She cursed again. This kind of thing was really frustrating.

Never mind. She could return to the story later. There wasn't a lot of time to lie around looking at her phone this morning, anyway. She needed to get into the office for a meeting at eight-thirty. Besides, it looked as though it might not be a bad day to be up and about. Sunlight was streaming into the bedroom and Kim could hear the chattering calls of a couple of kookaburras in the trees outside the apartment block.

As she got out of bed, she spotted the book which she had knocked to the ground and she felt a small pang of regret. She had started to read the biography of a well-known, and now sadly deceased, football manager some weeks before. It had landed on the floor face-up and the picture of the manager on the cover was a reminder of the interesting story which lay within, but which she had neglected in her preference for late night screen-time.

Kim picked the book up, noting that the bookmark was barely a quarter of the way through the pages. She resolved that tonight she would relax with some light reading, rather than the glow of the small screen.

After her shower, Kim went through to the open-plan kitchen and living space to make some breakfast. The TV remote was nowhere to be seen so she decided to put some music on instead; a set of speakers in the lounge could be used to stream music from a subscription service. She selected an album which her friend Paul had recommended to her last year during a holiday in London; a compilation of reggae tracks selected by DJ Derek. This was perfect music for a sunny morning.

Whilst she sat at the small table, eating some fruit and yoghurt, she browsed the sports results from the previous night on her tablet, which was propped up against a box-file. There wasn't much of note. The Big Bash cricket tournament had finished a couple of weeks earlier, as had the Australian Open tennis. Overseas, there were some interesting football results in the English FA Cup, with the two Manchester teams playing each other and Liverpool being beaten by a club from the lower leagues; one which included an Australian international in their team. Maybe this was a story which she could follow up on.

The little envelope icon at the bottom of the screen showed that there were three new emails to read. These would be personal emails as Kim had decided not to have access to her work email account on the tablet. It was good to have some small lines of separation between work and her life away from it, although it did feel as if these lines were slowly being eroded.

One of the new emails was marketing: an advertisement for a sale at the furniture store where she had bought her sofa. It seemed as though every time you bought anything these days you had to provide your email address so that you could be bombarded with the sort of crap which used to just be printed and shoved into letterboxes. Now there was e-crap as well as printed crap.

Next was an important mail from Chloe Clark, another contact in the UK, asking to arrange a time for the video call which they were planning. Kim would have to check her diary before responding to this so she set a reminder flag to prompt her to look at it again later that morning.

Lastly, there was a notification from OzTelia, the company which provided her phone line and broadband connection. She had missed paying a monthly bill and this email told her that she now had an 'overdue fee' to pay on top of the usual charges. While marketing emails were mildly irritating, this one was infuriating. She had no choice but to pay the fee before they tried to charge her even more.

Rummaging through the contents of her bag, she located her purse and extracted her credit card.

The email had a link to a payment page, but none of the details of the bill or her account were shown when it opened. They weren't making this easy.

Kim had to go back to her emails and

open the attachment which showed the bill, then flick between the document and the payment page, typing the relevant details into the various fields before making payment. She got there in the end but it could have been much simpler.

Along with the payment link, the email also suggested setting up Direct Debit so that future monthly payments would be made automatically. For once it seemed that they were trying to be helpful. It wasn't the first time Kim had forgotten a bill and been hit with a fee for an overdue payment. The email said that Direct Debits were 'quick and easy to set up' but when she looked at the clock on the kitchen wall, Kim realised she needed to get moving if she wanted to be on time for the meeting. Direct Debits would have to wait.

She grabbed her tablet, phone and purse, and dropped them into her bag, wincing slightly at the sharp sound which told her she had, yet again, dropped them on top of her voice recorder device. She made a quick check in the mirror in the hallway, straightening the shoulders of her dress and pinning back her hair, then headed for the door.

People and technology: A developing relationship

The start of Kim's day, or at least some elements of it, will probably be familiar to you. From our waking moments, much of what happens in our lives is dependent on, or assisted by, technology. Each day, we interact with mobile devices, computers, and internet-enabled objects. We use software packages and applications intended to provide us with information, to assist us with tasks, or to entertain us.

There has been a Digital Revolution which has profoundly affected many aspects of our lives; the way we work and the way we play, the way we communicate and socialise, how we find out what is (or is not) happening in the world, the way we buy and sell goods and services, our means of entertainment, how we manage our finances, how we travel, and the way we monitor our health. This list could extend into almost every facet of human life because technology is now intertwined with humanity.

Some of the technology which affects us is visible to us. Yet more is hidden from view. Many aspects of our lives are monitored, our actions recorded, and information gathered on our movements, behaviour and what we like and dislike. This data is used to make improvements in our lives, but also to influence us. Like it or not, we live in symbiosis with technology.

Sometimes, technology serves us well but sometimes it fails to do so, and it can fail in all manner of ways. Our relationships with technology are complex and built on many factors, our needs and desires changeable. When those needs and desires are not met, the consequences can be severe - a failure in software controlling life-support devices, for example - or simply a source of irritation, as illustrated by Kim's experiences with the advert on the news site, or the missing customer information for her phone bill.

Failures, in so far as we perceive them as failures, can result from poor design, or from some kind of error in the way technology was built, maintained, distributed or supported. In fact, any activity involved in the process of bringing us technology is subject to failure, because each element involves some degree of human endeavour, and humans are fallible. Technology is merely an instrument of human activity, provided by humans for humans.

However, an instance of a failure within technology does not necessarily mean it has failed us entirely. It can fail us in one or more ways whilst providing us with great value in others.

To further complicate matters, what may be valuable to one person may fail another, and what may be valuable at one time may lose its value later.

This is the predicament which faces those who work on providing technology products, or services underpinned by technology: how to provide the people who might use those products or services with what they need or want; how to foster and nurture a valued and trusting relationship between those people and the technology products they use.

Many organisations are conscious of, and attuned to, customer experience - the result of the interactions their customers have with them - and the touch points where those interactions occur. Technology increasingly influences those touch points. The relationship between the consumer and the technology products which they use can be critical in shaping their relationship with the organisations providing those products.

In considering those relationships, we are considering quality, a word which can be traced back to the Ancient Greeks and which many have attempted to define ever since. It is a word which has taken on great significance in the age of the consumer and yet it is a word which can cause confusion and misunderstanding. It is subject to many different interpretations.

Perhaps more than ever before, private companies, public

bodies and government departments are eager to focus on quality. But what does this really mean?

Kim is at the centre of our story, and the story will be at the centre of everything we discuss. We will see the part which technology plays in her life, how it affects her and those around her, and how her experiences make her feel. As we will see, if you want to provide technology for people, it makes sense to put those people at the centre of your thinking.

Chapter Two: On the way

Kim ran out of the flat and down the single flight of stairs to the air-conditioned lobby. The front doors of the building slid open and she was immediately hit by a blast of warm air. It was going to be a hot day in Sydney. The sunshine and blue skies were welcome but, when the temperature and humidity rose, life in the city could get uncomfortable.

As she reached the end of the street, Kim saw the queue at the bus stop. There were maybe fifteen people already waiting and she knew that at this time of day, and by this point in the journey, the buses could already be pretty full.

One of the benefits of her job was some flexibility around where and when she worked. On days like today, when she was needed in the office early, she felt grateful that she didn't have to go through this every morning, like so many other people heading into the city.

Taking up position at the back of the queue, Kim peered down the road to see whether a bus was on the way. The time she had spent paying the phone bill meant that she was cutting it fine if she wanted to get to work on time. The last thing she needed was to be stuck at a bus stop. Like the temperature, her stress levels were beginning to rise.

She sighed, frustrated. There was no sign of a bus. Pulling her phone from her bag, she opened the travel information app; one of the few which she used every day. As she travelled around the city, interviewing people and moving between her home and the office, she found it helpful to be able to search for transport options between different places, particularly when she was heading into areas she didn't know well. Most of all, she liked the real-time map which showed exactly where the buses, trains and ferries were on their journeys.

The map showed a bus just a couple of minutes away. Kim relaxed a little. Perhaps she would make the meeting after all. It wasn't that she was particularly keen to impress Jonny, her boss, but he never missed an opportunity to draw attention to people arriving late and she didn't want to give him the opportunity to make a crack at her expense.

The app was, as usual, spot-on. A bus appeared in the distance. As it pulled up to her stop, Kim noticed that the bus was quite empty. Despite this, it seemed to take the other passengers a little while to get on board, which was unusual. The process of getting people on and off the various modes of public transport had become much quicker and simpler since the city's transit department had introduced an electronic ticket system. By tapping a travel card (which looked similar to a credit card) on a card reader at the start and end of a journey, the correct fare was automatically deducted from a pre-paid balance. The need for tickets and cash had been eliminated.

It was a great system - unless, as seemed to be the case today, it wasn't working.

The card-reader machines were clearly experiencing some sort of problem. Usually their little screens showed messages which told passengers whether they had tapped their cards successfully, the balance remaining on the card, and the cost of each completed journey.

Unfortunately, the screens on this

particular bus were instead displaying some kind of error message:

CONNECTION FAILURE
>> ERR 34599
>> HOST UNREACHABLE

Just ahead of Kim, a young guy in a suit was looking around for some guidance. The bus driver, however, was staring straight ahead, eager to get moving.

"Excuse me," said the suit guy. He had a strong accent, maybe Eastern European.

The driver didn't respond, either because he hadn't heard, or more likely because he didn't want to engage with the confused passenger.

Suit guy tried again, a little louder this time

"Excuse me, please."

Begrudgingly, the driver looked at him. "What's up?"

"The machine is broken, I think. I cannot use my card."

The driver rolled his eyes. "Weren't you listening?" he said. "I told you all to just get on. The machine's out of order."

Clearly, the passengers at the front of the queue had asked the same question and the driver had given them some instructions, perhaps working on the principle that they would share the information with those outside the bus through some kind of collective intelligence.

Motivated by the driver's rudeness, and a growing feeling of irritation at the way the morning was going, Kim found herself getting involved in the conversation.

"We couldn't hear you. We were still out on the street. Do we not have to pay, then?"

"Well, unless you know how to fix it, it looks that way to me," replied the driver with a sarcastic smirk.

She shrugged her shoulders at the guy in the suit and smiled, gesturing for him to move towards the seats. As they made their way down the bus, Kim had to suppress a laugh as he expelled what were, judging by his tone, a selection of insults and profanities in his first language.

Kim took a seat and closed her eyes, taking a few deep breaths and trying to put aside the morning's frustrations, in preparation for the day ahead. After the weekly meeting, she wanted to continue work on an article she had been researching about the crossover between sport and video games. The time in the office could also be valuable in planning further work. Finding out what stories other people were working on sometimes prompted ideas for Kim. Listening to rumours or gossip from out in the field also helped. Sometimes these were worth investigating and developed into stories. Sometimes they were just fun to hear.

Her rumination was rudely interrupted by an electronic pinging sound. She looked at the source of the noise – the card-reader machine which had been out of action a few minutes earlier. The machine's screen had now lit up and was showing the more familiar message:

TAP YOUR CARD HERE
YOUR BALANCE IS: $0.00

A few of the other passengers had noticed, too, although most seemed to be pretending that they hadn't. After all, they were currently getting a free trip into the city and were keen to maintain that situation.

Kim, however, decided to do things by the book. Occasionally, ticket inspectors got on a bus and checked everybody's cards with some portable reader machines. If you hadn't registered for your journey, you could get a fine. At the very least, a conversation with an inspector would slow things down and put her at risk of missing the start of the meeting. Given how the day had gone so far, she wasn't taking any chances. She got out of her seat and tapped her card against the reader. Another pinging sound and a new message appeared:

CARD TAP SUCCESSFUL!
YOUR BALANCE IS: $32.50

Retaking her seat, she looked around at her fellow passengers. Almost everyone else on the bus was looking at an electronic device; checking social media or playing games, necks craned at an unnatural angle as they peered downwards. *Business must be good for chiropractors these days,* thought Kim as she put her headphones on, selected some relaxing music, and closed her eyes once more.

The bus continued its journey, express to the city now with no more stops before it reached Railway Square near Central Station. With the motion of the vehicle and the warmth of the sun through the window, Kim began to gently doze. When they arrived at their final stop, it took a few moments for her to collect her thoughts before she got up from her seat to disembark.

She retrieved her travel card from her bag and went to tap the card-reader at the front of the bus, but now the display screen was blank and it looked like the machine was switched off. There was no way to tap the card and tell the system that her journey had ended.

"The machine's not working again," she said to the driver.

"Doesn't matter. It wasn't working when you all got on."

"No... it came back on. I tapped my card. I need to tap again."

"Sorry, nothing I can do about it," came the reply. "I did tell you to just get on. Looks like everyone else had a free ride."

"But what do I do now?"

"No idea. You'll have to contact the ticket people."

Clearly the driver was going to be no help. Just when she had started to feel relaxed and calm, here was another little headache to deal with. This one would have to wait until later.

Kim stepped out onto the pavement, struck once more by the warmth of the air; a sharp contrast from the cooler environment of the bus.

The paper's offices were just a couple of blocks away. A quick glance at the clock display on the home screen of her phone told her that the bus had made good time. She could fit in a quick stop for a takeaway coffee. There were scores of cafés and outlets in this part of the city but her favourite was Café de Calidad; a small place which lay on the route between the bus stop and the office. It was little more than a kiosk really, run by a guy from Madrid called Mateo, but he certainly knew how to make great coffee.

She slid her phone into her bag and started walking. The streets were busy at this time of day and it was a challenge trying to manoeuvre along the crowded pavements when many of the people walking towards her were more intent on staring at their phones than looking where they were going. Spending a bus journey staring at their screens was one thing; walking into people whilst doing the same was just selfish. Kim tried to curb her annoyance. The problems she had experienced this morning were causing her to feel this way, but it would be a long day if she let every little thing irritate her.

As she got closer to 'Calidad', she spotted the unmistakeable figure of her colleague, Ian Ramsey, approaching from the opposite direction. Ian was tall and thin, with greying hair which he always kept very short. He was somewhere in his mid-forties, a family man, and had been with the paper for many years. As well as being a fellow sports correspondent, Ian was also a good friend, and – at least in the early stages of Kim's employment at the *Times* – he had been a mentor. He was always quick to ridicule that idea now, recognising that Kim's writing and ability to identify a good story were vital to the team on the Sports desk.

He spotted Kim and grinned. "Morning!" he said. "You managed to get yourself here in time. I'm impressed!"

"Only just. Who sets meetings for eight-thirty in the morning? Seriously."

"So you said last week… and the week before," Ian replied. "Some of us start work way earlier than this. You know why?"

"'News doesn't sleep'," they both said in unison.

This was a gentle dig at Jonny, their boss, and the person responsible for arranging the meeting. Jonny often used the phrase 'News doesn't sleep' when reminding the writers how important timekeeping and deadlines were in their line of work. Kim laughed, her mood lifting as she settled into the familiar rhythm of conversation with her friend.

"It's OK for you," she said. "You have kids to get you up nice and early. I have to rely on my personal motivation. That, and my phone. What are you doing here, anyway? Did you get lost? The office is the other way."

"Oh, I've already been in, but needed my morning coffee. I wanted to try this pre-order thing," replied Ian.

"What pre-order thing?"

"It's an app that Jonny showed me. You can order your coffee using the app and then you just turn up and pick it up."

"That's unlike you. I thought you were fighting the rise of the machines?"

Ian often told Kim that the machines were taking over and that they had to make a stand through affirmative action. He hadn't really come up with any good ideas yet. Using a road atlas rather than Google Maps on car journeys seemed like a futile gesture.

"I don't think this will be taking anyone's job," Ian grinned. "Anyway, I didn't have any cash on me and I can pay for it in the app."

"There's an ATM right there. You could have just got some cash!"

"Ah well," he shrugged, "I guess it was a bit of fun too."

Kim ordered her coffee. Sure enough, Ian's flat white was ready, but he waited with Kim and together they headed to the office and Jonny's meeting.

Technology development and the quest for quality

During her journey to work, Kim encounters and interacts with a range of technology products. Her experiences with them are as varied as the purposes of the products themselves. They have a direct bearing on her, albeit in relatively minor ways. There are no 'life or death' situations, but there are consequences - decisions are made, emotional responses are generated, and people's moods are affected.

Organisations which create and distribute these kinds of products would no doubt wish to provide their customers with a positive experience. They would hope that if their products were useful, reliable, and perhaps even enjoyable to use, this would create a good impression, not only of the technology but of their organisation as well.

Perhaps, on a more personal level, the people who work on the design, development, support and maintenance of the products may also be motivated to produce something which people liked and which made life easier.

In the case of Kim's travel planning app, they might well feel that they had been successful. Here is a software application which helps Kim on a daily basis, which she considers reliable, and which is likely to be useful to her for some time to come.

The electronic ticket system, usually reliable but failing on Kim's bus journey, shows that trust in technology (which may take time to establish) can be eroded. Perhaps the problem here, though, was not with the technology itself as much as the lack of support when it failed. If the bus driver had been able to provide some clear instruction and help to the passengers, maybe they would have been more forgiving of what seemed to be a temporary glitch. The human interaction around the electronic system - the knowledge and attitude of the driver - played a big part in the perception of the product as a whole.

Kim quickly formed an impression of the app which Ian was using to pre-order his coffee. She couldn't see any value in it, and she was quick to point this out to her colleague. Perhaps if she was feeling a little less frustrated, she might have been more open to the idea. Ian, meanwhile, had formed a different impression. For him, it was a novelty; a bit of fun. He might not have used it frequently, but if he got some pleasure from it perhaps the creators of the app might feel this was a success.

Companies and individuals alike, those responsible for the technology which Kim came across, would hope that their products generated a positive response. They would perhaps have discussed how best to provide their customers with a 'quality product' or a great customer experience. If there is a desire to do so; if companies invest time, effort and money in meeting these objectives, then why do they sometimes fall short? What are the challenges faced by the organisations, the teams and the people involved in technology work? In this section, we will look at some of the difficulties which they have to overcome, starting with an important question.

What is Quality?

If the quality of a product matters then it seems important that everyone involved in creating and maintaining that product understands what is meant by the word 'quality'. However, reaching a mutual understanding might not be easy.

In one sense, the question is easy to answer because, whilst we *might* be able to identify what quality means to others, each of us instinctively recognises quality from our own perspective. We know what we like and what we value.

We subconsciously assess quality as we use products or services. We may be preoccupied with a task we are carrying out, or with something entirely unrelated, but we form an impression of the product or service we are using nonetheless. This impression is subjective; influenced by our own unique blend of experiences and opinions, our needs and our mood.

Not only do we each assess the quality of products and services, we reassess their quality whenever we interact with them (although this may happen subconsciously and instantaneously). Our opinions, needs and moods change, sometimes over a prolonged period, or perhaps in an instant, with a single, decisive experience. Sometimes we are aware of these changes and sometimes they are so subtle that we don't notice them happening but because they occur, our perception of quality is variable.

There are external influences which might also be significant in our perception. Our own comparisons with other products and services might play a part, as may the opinions of others and the reports we receive from them. The extent to which such reports and opinions affect us is again dependent on a range of factors - the trust we place in the person from whom we hear them, the number of different people who provide such opinions, the consistency of the messages, and so on.

Once assessed or reassessed, an impression is established until the next interaction. In much the same way as a metal object can be formed, then melted down and recast, so our impression can be recast each time we interact.

It can therefore be said that quality is a subjective and variable impression of a product or service, instinctively reassessed and recast with each interaction.

This subjectivity and variability make the question of quality a complex one for the organisations which develop technology products, and for the people who work on these products. This brings us to their next challenge.

'The customer' does not exist

In our story, the coffee app which Ian uses generates different responses from different people. Where Kim is somewhat unimpressed and seemingly unlikely to use the app, Ian gives it a try after he is shown what it can do by Jonny (who we can assume viewed it in a positive light, given that he recommended it).

It isn't unusual in product development to hear customers - a group of people - referred to in the singular (for example in the phrase 'know your customer') but if each of us has, at any given time, our own perspective on quality, then there really is no such thing as 'the customer'. It may not always be clear who the potential customers are for a product. Even if it is reasonably clear who they are, each customer will assess quality in their own way: they will change their mind about what matters to them but may not always be aware of, or able to articulate, these changes. Meanwhile, uncontrollable external factors may affect the impression they form.

Finding common ground in the needs and desires of potential customers can establish the foundations for creating a popular and profitable product, yet common ground may not remain common; new technology and competing products may emerge, or social changes may occur, affecting the attitudes, needs and wishes of customers and causing them to diverge. These changes can happen rapidly, and a potential customer base can shrink or grow with them.

Beware of bias

It is not only customers who will have differing views on quality; so too will the people working on a product. Each of them may have a different interpretation of what quality means in the context of *this product* for *these customers*. Their interpretation will naturally be influenced by their own perspective and biases.

A cognitive bias represents an inclination towards a particular position or approach, based on a person's own beliefs or experiences, emotional responses, and other influences. Sometimes people can disregard information or evidence which conflicts with their own perceptions, or make assumptions based on personal observations, and this can in turn affect behaviour.

There are many different examples of cognitive biases (you can find some sources in the References and Further Reading section at the back of the book) and these can have a profound effect on the people involved in product development.

For example, some individuals may be subject to 'false-consensus bias'; a tendency to believe that their own preferences and values are shared by others. Their views on what might or might not be valuable to customers will be weighted towards their own beliefs. If they perceive something as useful, or appealing, they will be inclined to believe that customers will share the same viewpoint.

Another example of cognitive bias is the wonderfully named 'IKEA effect': the inclination to see greater value in something which we have a hand in creating. It can't be denied that assembling flat-pack furniture can present great challenges to some of us and it follows that, in the triumph of overcoming such difficulties, we might be duped into seeing elegance and style where none exists.

There are other potential pitfalls. Technology products, and the work associated with their creation, can be pioneering. As with any field where there is new ground to be broken, there are challenges in comprehending the implications and boundaries of discoveries. Understanding the capability of new technology, and the ways in which it could be applied, is not always straightforward.

What is more, for pioneers, the excitement at discovering something new can sometimes overwhelm; thoughts about whether to pursue some new discovery can be lost in the thrill of possibility.

There is a scene in the film *Jurassic Park* which neatly captures this risk. The scientist Dr Ian Malcolm (played by Jeff Goldblum) berates the park's creator, John Hammond (played by Sir Richard Attenborough), about the lack of respect for nature being shown in the creation of the dinosaurs which populate the theme park.

In reply to John Hammond's complaint that his team of scientists and their achievements are not being given due credit, Dr Malcolm answers that in being preoccupied with what they *could* do, the scientists never stopped to wonder if it was something that they *should* do.

As the scientists in *Jurassic Park* discovered, the belief that if something *can* be created then it *should* be (the 'Velociraptor Effect', perhaps) can sometimes have unintended and unpleasant consequences. The pioneering work in consumer technology has, at times, experienced similar problems. The results may not always be as dramatic (more rampant mediocrity than rampaging prehistoric carnivores) but in both cases, better conversations about the purpose and benefits of technology might have prevented some unloved and unwanted creations from being released.

The many challenges of technology work

If the previous passage seems critical, let me take a step back and state quite clearly that I understand that developing new technology can be difficult work. In spite of this, there are many excellent products which help people in many different ways, and which can provide people with fantastic experiences. When Kim wants to find the whereabouts of her bus during her journey to work, we see how the travel information app she uses helps; not only in finding that information, but presenting it in an engaging and relatable way.

The travel app may be the result of the work of a small group of people, or perhaps even one dedicated and talented developer. When larger groups of people come together to work on more complex systems, there are numerous diverse needs and challenges which must be considered and prioritised:

- **People.** First and foremost, the people working on the technology must be considered. They have lives away from this work, and their own needs and aspirations. Sometimes large numbers of people are involved in developing a product and it is not always easy to achieve a balance that suits all. Particularly when work is pioneering and time to market is key, people can be placed under great pressure. It can be mentally, emotionally and physically demanding.

- **Co-ordinating tasks.** Managing the interdependencies between activities, anticipating and resolving problems, building teams with the right combination of technical skills and interpersonal traits; there is much to consider and much which can go wrong.
- **Technical complexity.** The tools, methods, programming languages, data and infrastructure which support technology work must be understood and utilised correctly. Misuse or misunderstandings can have a profound effect on the resulting products and services.
- **Motive.** Familiarity with the desires of the people and organisations who request the work is crucial. The work is likely to be driven by a business idea or plan, or perhaps by legislation or regulation. In order to make a success of the endeavour, it is important that these factors are well understood.

This leads us to perhaps the biggest challenge in technology work.

The Communication Game

Very early in my career, I took part in an exercise which provided a simple but extremely effective demonstration of the difficulties in communicating with a group of colleagues.

The activity involved a group of ten people. Behind a screen, unseen, was a picture of a coat of arms; a shield shape divided into quadrants, with a banner underneath.

Each of the quadrants had an image in it: a boat, a castle, a lion, and the sun. The banner beneath displayed Latin words.

One member of the group was taken behind the screen and shown the picture, whilst the others sat around a large table and were each given a blank sheet of paper and a pen. The task for the person behind the screen was to relay a description of the image to the team in such a way that they could recreate it on their piece of paper.

There was a time limit, and of course revealing the image to the team was not permitted, but the team could ask questions of the unfortunate person who was describing the picture. That person became frustrated with the task and with the questions, which to them served to demonstrate that their colleagues were incapable of understanding simple instructions.

Of course, those colleagues were equally convinced that any difficulties being experienced were attributable to the incompetence of the person behind the screen. After all, they had the luxury of seeing the picture. How difficult could it be to describe it?

At the end of the exercise, we compared the original picture with the various efforts on display around the table. There were vast and sometimes comical differences.

Where some had attempted to draw with finesse and skill, others had regressed to their childhoods, with crude stickman pictures.

Shields, banners and quadrants were of different shapes and sizes. Pictures were in the wrong quadrants. Latin words were spelled incorrectly. There were rowing boats, sailing boats, and cruise ships. Lions, lionesses, and grotesque creatures which bore little resemblance to either.

We had castles with turrets, castles with moats, and castles with kings and queens sitting serenely on thrones in the courtyard. There were bright, blazing suns, clouds with the sun emerging from behind, and smiling suns wearing sunglasses.

In almost all cases, the pictures had been embellished with details which were never mentioned during the exercise.

As a recent starter in my first job with a software house, I had been given a perfect example of what I would see in technology projects over the next two decades.

The sad truth is that when it comes to understanding and communicating the intended purpose of products, teams of technology professionals often struggle.

In fact, the reality is somewhat worse, because in software projects the intended purpose can, and does, change as we go. When this happens, the communication problem is exacerbated.

To make the exercise even more revealing (and realistic), it would have been helpful if the picture was changed partway through describing it: "The lion is actually a tiger. The shield isn't a shield anymore, it's a circle shape instead. Oh, and would you mind changing those words from Latin to French? Actually, forget it, I've decided I don't need a coat of arms after all."

This is how product development works, and for some of the organisations and people involved in software development, painful lessons sometimes have to be learned from failed projects or mismatched solutions in order to understand this, and to develop the means to react to such demands.

Self-inflicted wounds

Understanding purpose and agreeing on objectives is just one example of communication problems. There are many others. In fact, technology projects are often immersed in them, and some of the wounds are self-inflicted:

- **Geographically dispersed teams.** People in different locations (sometimes even different time zones) working on different, but heavily interdependent elements of products.
- **New terms and phrases.** These crop up across the industry with bewildering frequency, and are rapidly adopted by those who might not fully understand them but are keen to be seen as trail-blazers in their field. Words can be used in mysterious ways. For example, it is quite normal in software development projects for tasks to be carried out to determine whether things are working from a 'non-functional' standpoint.

- **TLAs (three letter acronyms).** A badge of honour to some who see them as removing the need for fuller, more descriptive terms which might be of help to people who are less familiar with a concept.
- **Grand and lengthy job titles.** Often preceded with the word 'Senior', these only serve to confuse others as to what exactly the person does.

A fog of confusion swirls around the people, their purpose, and the products they work on. At times, it appears this lack of clarity is quite deliberate, for these are devices which can be used to differentiate technology workers from their peers, to elevate them to the status of 'expert', regardless of their actual expertise.

It is little wonder that under such circumstances there is often a failure to reach a common understanding of why a particular piece of work is required and what is being done: when, where and by whom.

If the people with technical knowledge and skills who are working together cannot effectively communicate with each other, what hope is there of communicating effectively with people who have no such technical knowledge or skills? Where does this leave the client or customers?

Responding to change

The need to address communication problems, whether relating to clarity and shared understanding within teams, or how to react to customers and their changing needs, has not gone unnoticed.

Better communication has been one of the principal considerations in a number of techniques and methods which have been shaped and refined by people involved in technology work. The eagerness of organisations to adopt Agile and Lean ways of working is testament to the longstanding ineffectiveness of many technology teams to fulfil the needs of those organisations.

The *Manifesto for Agile Software Development* (more commonly known as the *Agile Manifesto*), written in 2001, captured the ideas and principles which underpin Agile development, among them an emphasis on collaboration between the people responsible for technology, in order to better address the needs of customers; to deliver products which are valuable to them.

Lean principles, meanwhile, focus on the elimination of waste from development processes, and on continuous analysis and improvement of those processes in order to improve the quality of products. Emerging from Japanese manufacturing methods, Lean has been adapted for software development with variations targeted at large enterprises and smaller start-up organisations. Central to these is the feedback loop of learning, building and measuring, to determine whether products are useful and interesting to the people who might use them. As with Agile development, Lean has a clear emphasis on customers, and on providing products which will satisfy them.

A relentless move towards these practices has been a significant trend in software development activity. The methods, and the associated cultural changes which are often required within organisations, promote iterative ways of working, with an emphasis on delivering less complex products, often to test customer response before making adjustments. The techniques encourage regular feedback from customers, and rapid response to that feedback; refining ideas and revisiting design and development activities with the intention of delivering products which better reflect what customers want:

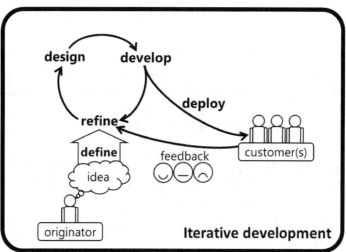

This is in contrast with the more linear and sequential approaches previously favoured by many in software development:

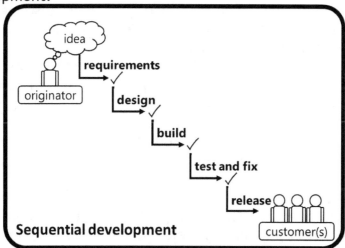

Sequential models such as Waterfall or V-Model rely on intensive periods of collecting and refining requirements for a product before design and development activity can take place. Products developed using these models are intended to be complete when released to customers. Central to the approach is an assumption that by adhering to the requirements captured at the outset, the product will fulfil the wishes of those customers.

The more iterative approaches allow organisations to adopt strategies with different attitudes towards the risk associated with releasing to customers. Such strategies depend on the product's purpose, the objective of a release, and the organisation's ability to respond to feedback:

- **Piloting a product.** If the release instigates some sort of experiment, 'beta phase', or pilot with a limited number of prospective customers, they may have greater tolerance for incomplete or immature elements of the product. The organisation providing it may feel comfortable that the product is made available with known problems, and an acceptance that prior testing of the product has been limited.
- **Monitoring a released product.** Even when a product is made available to a broad group of customers, an organisation may feel confident in their means of monitoring what happens, and their ability to rapidly update or fix the product based on observations. Again, this may mean that they are prepared to compromise on prior testing or are willing to resolve known problems and add delayed features later.
- **Releasing a 'finished' product.** In the case of products which are unlikely to be updated for some time, which customers will expect to be rich in working features, or where problems or faults will have profound consequences, the tolerance for untested features or known problems may well reduce. In some cases, there may be legislation or regulation, such as Disability

Discrimination laws or financial reporting requirements, which affect that tolerance.

Given that Agile and Lean methods have been so widely adopted, this would suggest that customers should be feeling increasingly happy with the technology products emerging. If customers and value are now at the heart of technology work, there must surely be a greater perception of quality.

Perhaps this is the case, and perhaps not. There may be more that can be done to understand what really matters to the people like Kim who are using that technology.

Chapter Three: Things to do

"We're all busy people. We all have things to do, but it's important to be here for the start of the meeting. In our work, we can't afford to be late because, as I think I've mentioned before, news doesn't sleep."

Jonny Wilson's catchphrase prompted a groan from some of the gathered writers who made up the *Sydney Times'* Sports desk. Kim noticed that Andy, the junior who had arrived a few minutes late and prompted Jonny's comments, was looking down at his feet, no doubt feeling a little self-conscious but also perhaps suppressing a smile at the reaction to Jonny's comments.

Jonny was the Sports Editor and, in part due to his close relationship with the paper's editor, he was a prominent person at the *Times*; part of a small group who had inside knowledge of important management decisions and the strategy of the owners. His fondness for making jokes, coupled with a self-confidence which he didn't always remember was not shared by all those around him, could sometimes lead to insensitivity in the way he dealt with others. One evening over drinks with the team, Kim had spoken to him about this, and he had promised to try to rein in the wisecracks, and to avoid giving people a hard time in front of their colleagues. Clearly, he needed to try a little harder.

Kim got on well with Jonny, and generally enjoyed working with him. They were around the same age and had been working together for a couple of years, after he had come to the paper from an Auckland-based daily. He had a quite different style from Norman White, the previous Sports Editor. Where Norman was interested in details, sometimes drawing criticism from the journalists for micro-managing their work, Jonny liked to keep his involvement to a minimum. In his own words, he liked to "steer things" or "point people in the right direction". He had a knack for reducing complex subjects to short statements or comments.

Sometimes this worked well and other times people longed for more information. Kim liked the freedom which came with Jonny's approach, but sometimes wished for a little more clarity about what he actually wanted.

As usual, his weekly update covered a few of the previous week's highlights: mentions for stories which had been favourably received or had generated a reaction in social media – along with some ideas for stories which might take the spotlight in the coming days. This week there were also two items of general interest: a vague update on the technical problems that had affected the system they used for submitting articles ("they'll get it sorted this week"), and a brief summary of the circulation figures which had been reported the previous day ("pretty crap").

The weekly meeting was different to the daily editorial meetings where they talked about which stories would run in the paper and online, and how prominent they would be. During that meeting, the writers often pitched ideas for feature stories which could run alongside breaking news and sports results. Those discussions were usually interesting, but the more mundane weekly ones often caused Kim's attention to drift elsewhere. On this occasion, her gaze was drawn towards the view of Darling Harbour and a fond but patchy memory of a drunken evening spent on a harbour cruise. She was brought abruptly back to the here and now by Jonny's voice.

"… so, Kim and Ian, I'd like you to come along, please. Can you both make it?"

"No problem for me," replied Ian

Unaware of when and where her presence was requested, but keen to avoid admitting to daydreaming, Kim bluffed an answer. "Yes, that should be fine. I'll just double-check my calendar after this."

Jonny gave her a strange look, perhaps realising that she hadn't been listening, but he managed to resist the temptation to make a joke at her expense.

Once the meeting was over, she asked Ian what Jonny had been talking about.

"It's a meeting this afternoon with a company called AI-Bel who have some software which he wants us to look into," he explained. "I don't know too much more about it. Where had you drifted off to, anyway?"

"Oh, I don't know," replied Kim. "I was just thinking about something. You know how it is in Jonny's meetings."

"I do, only too well. Don't worry about it. I'm not sure Jonny really noticed,

and we've got some time to look into it.
I'll find out what I can and we can talk
it through. Coffee and a chat later?"

"Sure," Kim replied, smiling at the way
Ian slipped into his supportive,
mentoring role. "We can catch up before
the meeting."

Kim found a workspace in 'The Stadium';
an area of the office with a few banks of
hot-desks for sports writers to use. When
the office space had been rearranged,
someone had come up with the idea of
naming the different areas according to
the kind of stories which the people who
would be sitting there worked on. The
Finance writers worked in 'The Pit',
named after the old trading pits of Stock
Exchanges, the political writers were in
'Parliament', and so on. It was intended
to be fun but some of the old-school
journalists found it puerile. They also
resented losing their allocated desks.

Kim connected her laptop to the screen
on the desk. Mercifully, there were no
operating system updates to install so
she was soon ready to start work.

Unfortunately, her mind was racing,
with different thoughts swirling around
and competing for attention; not all
relating to work. If she was to get into
the right frame of mind, she needed to

eliminate some of the distractions.

She formed a mental to-do list.

There was some preparation to be done for the meeting with AI-Bel, but she could leave that until she caught up with Ian just before they went in. Better for them to go through it together.

Then there was the confusion over the electronic ticket on this morning's bus journey to sort out, and those emails which she had been looking at over breakfast. The one from Chloe Clark had been important, so that seemed a good place to start.

Chloe was Editor of an independent magazine in the UK called *Two Halves*. It was a well-established publication which had been running for over twenty years and had a growing audience subscribing to an online edition. The magazine focused on football and, where it had once been devoted to the clubs and leagues in the UK, it now featured many stories relating to the global game.

Kim's friend Paul worked for the magazine and it was while she was staying with him during her visit to London the previous year that he had floated the idea of Kim taking up a role with the magazine. He had spoken to Chloe, who had seemed keen to bring Kim in.

At first, Kim had dismissed the idea,

being reluctant to consider leaving a large daily newspaper for something which she considered less prestigious. She didn't tell Paul this was the reason, instead saying that she wanted to continue her involvement in a broader range of sports.

Over the last couple of months, however, she had started to give it serious consideration. Some of the changes at the *Times* had led to a strained atmosphere, with growing resentment of the new generation from the older hands. The circulation figures were a constant source of discussion and there had been rumours that the owners may even consider becoming an online-only publication. Not that this in itself troubled Kim - she was familiar with modern digital editing and publishing methods, and generally felt positive about the new ways of working. But the uncertainty at the paper was making people feel unsettled and morale was low.

So far, Kim and Chloe had only been in touch via email but Kim had agreed to have a video call with Chloe, to see what she had to say about the magazine and what kind of work might be available. Kim's working theory was that they might need someone to report on the leagues in Australia, also to write feature articles on the growth of the game in this region. Chloe seemed interested in the work Kim had done with the *Times* website team, and in her activity on social media sites, as much as in her writing. Maybe they wanted to grow their digital presence and expand coverage in Australia and Asia.

Chloe was very keen to have the video call and was pushing for this week. As Kim looked at her calendar she saw that, as usual, most of her evenings would be busy with interviews or attendance at sporting fixtures, but Thursday night was an exception. Kim replied to Chloe, suggesting that they talk at nine o'clock Sydney-time on Thursday evening, which would be mid-morning in the UK. She also sent a short email to Paul, asking if he knew anything that might be useful for Kim in advance of the call.

With these two messages sent, the next email caught Kim's attention - the reminder from OzTelia, the phone company. The bill was paid but there was still the Direct Debit to set up. She clicked on the link in the email and a web browser window opened.

It seemed as though setting up a Direct Debit should be a relatively simple process but the website was apparently created with a secondary purpose as a kind of psychological test. She remembered a lecturer at university who had showed them something called the 'Five Room Puzzle'; a challenge where you were shown a plan of a house with five rooms and asked to draw a single continuous line which crossed each of the walls just once.

It was an ingenious, devious device, intended to frustrate, and ultimately to force the students to accept that there was no legitimate solution. For a group of smart people who liked to solve problems, this was not easy. It was, however, perfect preparation for the experience of using OzTelia's website.

Much like the puzzle, it had looked deceptively easy at first. The section of the website for Direct Debits gave a choice of options: Setup, Amend, or Cancel. Selecting the first of these led to a login page with some instructions about what to do once she had logged in. Of course, once she had logged in, the instructions disappeared, which made things a little complicated.

Kim opened another tab in the browser and found the instructions again. Unfortunately, the words and pictures which described the account page and the steps to follow were very different to what she saw on her own screen. There was no sign of a link to create a Direct Debit anywhere but there was a little picture of the company's mascot; a kind of cartoon mobile phone called Ozzie, which she remembered from their TV ads. Ozzie had a little speech bubble saying: 'Need help?'. She most certainly did.

When she clicked on the picture of Ozzie, a 'Support' page appeared, containing a long list of possible topics to read. There was no time to read through them all but the page also had a place to search for a term so she typed 'Direct Debit' and hit the button. A picture appeared of Ozzie riding a bike, with an animated spinning circle around him and the words 'Working on it...' underneath.

After a few seconds, a familiar sight. The search had taken her back to the page with options to Setup, Amend or Cancel; the same place where the process had started. This was no help at all. Surely it was possible to talk to someone instead.

After a bit of digging around, Kim found a page called 'Getting in touch with us'. It looked like there were different paths to follow, depending on what you wanted to talk to them about. One of the options was Billing, and this led to another list of choices. About halfway down that list she spotted 'Setting up your Direct Debit'. She selected it.

After a short interlude during which

Ozzie once more appeared on his bike, the screen showed those same three options: Setup, Amend, and Cancel. It didn't seem to matter what she did. It was her destiny to return to this page.

Suddenly, a box popped up on the screen:

>> Hi, this is Jim. Can I help you with anything today?

She'd seen this sort of thing before; a kind of chat support where they tried to help you without actually talking to you. Ian had told her that they were not real people she was chatting with but some kind of automated response system. It was worth a try:

>> Hi Jim. I'm trying to set up a Direct Debit but I can't work out how to do it

A short delay, then:

>> I can help you with this. Who am I chatting with?
>> My name is Kim
>> Hi Kim. And you need help with a Direct Debit?
>> Yes
>> OK. There are three options for Direct Debits. You can Setup, Amend or Cancel. Which of these would you like to do?
>> Setup
>> Great. Can you please tell me what sort

of service you have with us. Mobile, home phone or broadband.

>> Home phone and broadband

>> Is this an ADSL or Cable connection?

>> I'm not sure… Cable I think

>> Unfortunately there is no facility for setting up Direct Debit online for Cable customers. Please call us and we can set this up for you over the phone.

Kim closed the chat window in frustration. What a waste of time. Why send out an email telling her to set up Direct Debit online if she couldn't do it, and why didn't the website tell her which customers could or couldn't do it? Now she would have to try to find a phone number to call them and would probably have to sit on hold for twenty minutes. Maybe another day.

She felt a little guilty about shutting down the chat with Jim mid-conversation, but if Ian had been right and Jim really was just a robot then she probably hadn't hurt his feelings too much.

Empathy: the essential ingredient

If you use technology, there is a good chance that at some time or another you will have had a similar experience to Kim. Carrying out a seemingly simple task – in this case, setting up a direct debit for a phone bill – is thwarted by a website which has been designed and built in such a way that the task becomes prohibitively difficult.

The frustration Kim feels is largely down to the content of the site, and the poorly defined links which repeatedly send her back to the same page. But when she finds herself in difficulty, she also feels unsupported. The site's support pages are no help whatsoever and the chat system, whilst finally providing some kind of explanation, does little to improve Kim's mood (or her impression of the website and the company). She notices some of the visual elements which have been included, perhaps in an attempt to enliven what might be rather mundane activities, but animated pictures of cartoon mobile phones do not compensate for being unable to do the thing you set out to do.

During her efforts, Kim is reminded of an unsolvable puzzle and sometimes it can indeed feel as though these sorts of difficulties are the result of some cruel trick; a deliberate attempt to frustrate us through the use of deception and misinformation. It would be an unusual (and probably unemployed) designer who set out to create such a troubling product. Poor experiences are less likely to be by design than the result of errors, bad decisions, poor management, or a combination of these.

Perhaps Kim has little option but to continue using OzTelia's products and services, regardless of how ineffective they are. It might be that they operate in a market with few competitors and have little incentive to change or to think about how people will feel when they use their products. Kim's experience suggests that, in the design of their website at least, the company has not shown the care and consideration their customers would hope for.

In this section, we will explore how empathy – the ability to see things from another person's perspective – can help people involved in product development to consider the people who use those products, and help companies like OzTelia create better experiences for their customers. We will look at some of the techniques used in software development which have contributed to an empathy gap, and some methods which have been adopted in an attempt to close that gap.

A lesson from history

During my teenage years, I was given a lesson in the power of empathy. My family had moved to a new city and I had moved to a new school. It was an important time for me in many ways, not least of which was my education. I was about to enter the last two years of schooling, the period when my marks contributed to the final grades I would receive.

Whilst some of the subjects I would study were mandatory, I had the opportunity to elect others. The selection mechanism meant that I had to decide between subjects from various groups: two from the Sciences, one from Humanities, and so forth.

My criteria for deciding were not entirely logical and dispassionate. A bad experience with dissection of frogs meant that Physics got the nod over Biology, and a particularly tedious lesson in rock formations probably edged out Geography in favour of History.

History was not a subject which I had shown any great interest in, or aptitude for, up to that point. This changed during our first lesson with my new teacher, when she explained her teaching philosophy to the class. In particular, she emphasised the importance of empathy, which she said was central to the way we would learn. She even wrote the word on the blackboard in big letters to help us remember. It certainly stuck in my mind.

Our teacher went on to describe how we could better understand the events we would learn about by placing ourselves in the position of the people who witnessed them, or in some cases by hearing from those people.

The subject matter was the Second World War, and over the following weeks we watched several episodes of the documentary series *The World at War*, produced in the 1970s by Jeremy Isaacs.

This was a landmark documentary series, and perhaps its greatest strength was its ability to provide an insight into the experiences of the people who lived through the events leading up to the Second World War, how the conflict affected their day-to-day lives, and the consequences for them in the years that followed.

Interviews were used as a technique to capture their recollections but also, crucially, their emotional responses. We could see the pain in their eyes and hear their voices breaking. We could begin to comprehend the sadness and despair of victims, or the guilt or defiance of perpetrators of violent acts and unspeakable atrocities.

As a student of this period of human history, I was immediately captivated by the idea of putting myself in the shoes of these witnesses. Hearing their voices and stories, and seeing how they were affected, was a world away from my previous experience of History lessons; endless lists of events, dates and numbers, and little more than a memory exercise.

Which year did Charles II become King of England? When was the Magna Carta signed? How many troops were involved in the D-Day landings? These are things which I was taught but which I could only now answer after a quick Google search or a visit to Wikipedia. But ask me how the Allied soldiers *felt* as they arrived in landing craft on the beaches of Normandy in June 1944 and I can tell you that they were terrified of what lay in wait, but elated to be leaving the small vessels which had been tossed around on the English Channel during the crossing. Some were simply happy to get back on dry land, despite the dangers ahead. I remember this because I heard it from those who were affected.

Facts and figures might not convey real experiences but hearing people's stories connects us to them. Their feelings and emotions foster empathy, and help us to understand their responses.

Quantifying Quality

If stories and feelings tell us more about human responses than cold facts, dates and numbers, this might provide a clue as to why software development teams, and the organisations they work with, sometimes struggle with the question of quality.

In this field, refuge is often sought in numbers. As discussed earlier in the book, it can be challenging to reach an understanding of what quality means. Perhaps in an attempt to make this task simpler, to reach a consensus among those involved, there is a tendency to attempt to quantify quality.

By setting numeric quality targets - sometimes called exit criteria - a desired state can be agreed upon; a point at which the product is deemed good enough for whatever follows, including whether it is ready to be released to customers. The numbers act as a comforting security blanket, creating a sense of control. Even if the picture they paint is troubling, at least they provide a means of seeing that picture.

Unfortunately, whether the picture is troubling or not, it may well be a misrepresentation. Common metrics such as counting test cases passed and failed, or counting defects, are unreliable, given that they rely on equivalence (each item counted being of the same value or significance) and ignore subjectivity (what you consider acceptable, I might consider unacceptable). They are also very limited representations, excluding crucial information which is not, or cannot be, counted. For example, a count of test cases does not represent all the testing which occurs as it excludes exploratory or investigative work beyond the narrow confines of those test cases, and a count of defects excludes problems found and fixed without ever being recorded. Not to mention that the numbers tell us nothing about aspects of the product which have not been tested, and problems which may yet be found.

Quality is not measurable in the way cost or time might be measured. If we accept that quality is subjective and variable, how can it be a fixed attribute which can be counted? Cost can be measured in units of currency: dollars and cents, pounds and pence. Time can be measured in units of hours, days or weeks. There is no such unit of measurement for quality.

This is not to dismiss metrics entirely. Whilst they cannot be treated as absolute measures of quality, some can be useful and a range taken together can, if treated with care, be a helpful tool in identifying patterns and potential problems. I have myself spent time carefully preparing reports containing metrics (including those mentioned here), thinking such reports were helpful. To an extent they were; however, their value lay not in the numbers but in the conversations which they triggered; about what the metrics really told us and, crucially, what they did not tell us. These discussions with people who had an interest in the quality of the software (especially those who made decisions about whether software was ready to be released), whilst more challenging than simply pulling numbers from a spreadsheet or a database, required an understanding of the story behind the numbers and what the implications might be for the people who were going to use the software.

As difficult as it might sometimes be, the less time and effort spent trying to quantify quality, and the more spent talking about quality, the better. Numbers might tell us *something* about products, but not *everything*, and metrics; even combinations of metrics with clear patterns, offer no guarantees about the impression customers will form of technology. As I discovered in my History lessons, and the conversations triggered by my work reports, storytelling can be far more effective in understanding human responses and how others see things.

Mind the gap

The connection which stories can create helps us to address the empathy gap which can occur when one party is unable to understand how another party might feel in a given set of circumstances. Such a gap can easily occur in the development of products such as OzTelia's website; internally, between those working together, and externally, between those people and their customers.

When there is pressure to deliver a new product, or to make important changes, we may lose sight of the pressure that colleagues are under, perhaps becoming critical of their decisions or efforts. This can be exacerbated when there is miscommunication and misunderstanding around the objectives of the work, the business benefits, and the judgement of what matters to customers.

That judgement may be flawed if customers have not been consulted, or techniques applied which help capture their point of view. Understanding who customers might be and how they could get value from a product is crucial in the quest for quality.

It is worth emphasising that this does not mean that customers always know best when it comes to designing products, or that radical and innovative thinking on the part of product designers cannot lead to wonderful, useful and valuable products.

The importance of innovation in providing people with something they come to value can be seen in products such as the Ford Model T and, a century later, the iPod. Yet these famous inventions were not borne from a conscious effort to bypass customers or a feeling that designers knew best. Quite the opposite, in fact - they resulted from a deep empathy with real people, the problems those people faced, and how their lives could be improved.

Henry Ford recognised that people wanted a fast, affordable, and maintainable method of transportation. He knew that families and individuals alike would relish the opportunity to own a car like the Model T and he also understood the freedom which it represented.

Apple, where Sir Jonathan Ive designed the iPod, knew that people wanted a portable means of storing and listening to music; something which had capacity for their music collections but which was lightweight and simple to use.

At Apple, the freedom to experiment and innovate came from the top of the organisation, and an understanding that great products can result from thinking about customers first. At a presentation to a large group at Apple's Worldwide Developer Conference (WWDC) in 1997, Steve Jobs, the company's CEO explained his philosophy:

"One of the things I've always found is you've got to start with the customer experience and work backwards to the technology... What incredible benefits can we give to the customer? Where can we take the customer? Not start with 'let's sit down with the engineers and figure out what awesome technology we have and how we are going to market it.'"

This attitude probably helps explain, in part at least, some of the achievements of that company over subsequent years. It would be wrong to suggest that Apple always get things right but, when they do, they design and build spectacularly successful and popular products which many of their customers love.

Degrees of separation

It isn't always easy for those who work on the development of technology to empathise with their customers, particularly if they have little direct interaction with them. Whether by accident or design, opportunities for development teams to interact directly with customers can be scarce. In 1929, the Hungarian writer Frigyes Karinthy described the theory of 'Six Degrees of Separation'; the idea that any two people can be connected to each other through a chain of six or fewer steps. In software development, it can sometimes feel as though those degrees of separation are actively maintained between customers and the technical people working on products for them.

Instead, techniques and methods have been used which are intended to bridge the gap; to capture what those customers want, to distil and refine these desires and to relay them to technical people.

For many years, the dominant method used in software development was written requirements, captured in documents which were often extensive and weighty. The premise that these documents accurately capture the needs and desires of customers underpins this method. The theory is that through requirement document reviews and rework it is possible to reach an accord on what a product should be like; how it should behave and operate. The documents can be passed on to those tasked with building, testing, supporting and maintaining the product and a shared understanding can be reached.

Following this approach means that those people need not concern themselves with why this work is required - technical people can instead focus their energies on what they are building and how to do it. This way, customer empathy is lost. Concern for adherence to process overtakes concern for what people might actually want. If the product is built in such a way that it does what the requirements state, and if it can be demonstrated that it does so, then (so the theory goes) it will meet the needs of customers. Unfortunately, the reality is often quite different.

It is not difficult to imagine that this kind of approach might have been adopted in the development of the OzTelia website which caused Kim so much frustration. There could have been an extensive exercise in gathering, documenting, reviewing and reworking requirements. These requirements may have been translated into technical specifications and passed on to development teams, who were asked to build the different components of the website according to those specifications. Testers were very likely asked to do little more than confirm that what had been built conformed to the specifications. Little consideration would be given to customers like Kim, or their experience whilst using the website (although there would no doubt be some metrics which would reassure everybody involved about the quality of the product).

The consequences of relying on written requirements can go further than the effect on customers. Requirements can be ambiguous and inconsistent, and can be interpreted differently by different people. They may not even feel that they have the time (or inclination) to properly read and absorb them. As work on the product continues and new information or ideas come to light, the requirements can change. Misunderstandings occur and cause inefficiency as people attempt to reach a consensus. This in turn causes delays and inflated costs, which can result in projects being abandoned. If a product is ultimately delivered, often later than planned, it may be a product which:

- Fails to capture what was intended in the first place.
- Has taken so long to produce that it is no longer wanted or needed.
- Has been beaten to market by a rival product.

For public sector organisations, such an outcome can lead to poor services and great costs for taxpayers, embarrassing political failures, inquiries and investigations. In the commercial sector, a poorly received product can be the difference between a company's success or failure, perhaps affecting their value, share price, reputation, the jobs of people working there (whether they were directly involved in the product development or not) and, in some cases, the continuing existence of the organisation.

There are numerous examples of failed technology projects which were either cancelled or subject to lengthy delays and huge increases in costs. In a climate where schedules are likely to be missed and costs spiralling out of control, a 'blame culture' can emerge. Consideration for how a product will be received can slip down the list of priorities. People will be more interested in putting themselves out of the firing line than into the shoes of customers.

Naturally, those whose ideas and business strategies instigate work on such projects, and those who control the budgets associated with these endeavours, have asked whether there is a better way to deliver products and change. Frustrated and unfulfilled technology workers have asked the same thing. After all, there is little pleasure in working in an environment of confusion and blame, where goals are not achieved and customers and clients are dissatisfied.

From these frustrations and questions, from a recognition that large complex releases have not always been in the interests of many organisations, their employees or their customers, the methods associated with Agile and Lean development have emerged and proliferated.

Closing the gap

As we covered earlier, Agile and Lean practices are intended to help deliver value to customers. In order to do so, there is a recognition that more effective methods are needed to address the separation of customers from the people working to develop products for them.

An example is the Scrum Framework; an approach which involves development teams working in short, focused sprints on features prioritised by a Product Owner. The Product Owner is the link between customers and the development team, defining the list of product features, and signing off on products when they are satisfied that the required work has been done. The approach replaces detailed requirements with more succinct User Stories, intended to explain who might want to use a product and describe what they might want to use it for.

The role of Product Owner is one which requires deep customer empathy, an intimate understanding of their needs and desires, and an ability to express these effectively. Because this model maintains a degree of separation between customers and the development team, the Product Owner's ability to communicate with both is crucial. If they are not effective in this regard, if they have not really understood customers' desires, then they simply become the mechanism by which those desires are miscommunicated.

A crucial element of the Lean approach, meanwhile, is the idea of a Minimum Viable Product (MVP), to be provided to customers, or prospective customers, in order to obtain feedback and refine the product (or perhaps abandon it if feedback indicates that it will not ultimately be something which people want).

Feedback can be elicited in many ways. Examples include:

- Observation of customers using a product, the way it is used, and the responses and reactions generated.
- Monitoring of visitors to web pages where customers can sign up for a product.

- A/B testing, which compares reactions and responses to two different versions of the product.
- Responses provided by customers to support teams and other customer-facing staff.
- Customer interviews where people speak about their experiences, expressing what they liked and didn't like about a product.

This last technique demonstrates how customer empathy can be applied in a direct and meaningful way. There may still be hurdles to overcome in reaching a shared understanding with the customer, and in relaying findings to different people working on the product, but the methods make it easier for everybody involved to hear the customer's voice and to ask them about their responses.

Other simple and practical steps can be taken to foster empathy. For example, encouraging people involved in the design and development of applications and websites to try using their product with a phone's accessibility features enabled, or on a computer with only a keyboard attached, can help them to better understand the experience for customers with visual impairments or an inability to use a mouse. Meanwhile, asking the people who develop an organisation's applications and systems to spend time sitting alongside colleagues who operate those systems allows them to observe how they are actually used, the features which are popular (as well as those which are ignored), and the problems caused by some aspects of the design.

Simple exercises such as these can provide designers and developers with real insight into what their work means for other people. Changes to systems, websites and applications can be made with those people, their needs, and the way they act in mind.

A final thought on the empathy gap. Sometimes overlooked is the simple fact that the people working on products are consumers of technology themselves. In some cases, they may use the very product they are working on in their day-to-day lives. If not, they are likely to find similarities between that product and other things they use.

These similarities could be in the way products look, how they respond to certain actions, how easy or difficult it is to carry out tasks, or how those tasks are supported. Knowing what they like or don't like, and what works or doesn't work well for them, can be a great benefit. It doesn't mean that their personal preferences always represent the best path to follow but if something feels wrong, or their emotional response suggests a possible problem for customers, this is worthy of attention. It might just be the simplest way to bridge the gap.

Chapter Four: Rise of the machines

Ian looked miserable. Kim could see him waiting for her as she made her way from the lifts to the café in the lobby of their building. He had found a table and was sitting with his laptop in front of him. They had arranged to meet there to have a quick chat about the meeting they were going to that afternoon. It looked as though he had already ordered a drink - the coffee wasn't as good here as the stuff from Café Calidad, but Ian already knew that so there must be some other explanation for the glum expression on her colleague's face.

"What's up?" asked Kim, taking a seat opposite him.

"It's this meeting. Have you had a look

at this company's website?"

"You mean AI-Bel? No, I haven't yet. Who are they?"

"They produce software which automatically writes articles. You remember when there were those rumours about the job losses on the Finance desk?"

Kim nodded slowly, feeling a little uncomfortable about the way the conversation was going.

"That was around the time they brought in AI-Bel," continued Ian. "They asked them to help with reports on Financial figures and that sort of thing. I just had a chat with Sam on the Finance Desk and she told me that the writers up there thought that the software was brought in to cut costs... that they would end up losing their jobs."

"But that hasn't happened, has it?"

"Well... no," conceded Ian. "I mean not yet, anyway. But it's a pretty big worry for them. It seems so far-fetched... automated writing."

"So, what does this have to do with Sport?" asked Kim.

"I don't really know. I guess there is some plan to use it with us, too. It can't be good though, can it?"

"Let's not get ahead of ourselves. You'd better show me this website so I can see what we're heading into."

They made their way back up to the 24th floor and into the boardroom. Kim had noticed that Jonny liked to use the boardroom for meetings when the executives weren't around. Perhaps it was the big leather seats, or the expansive views towards the city, with the top of the Harbour Bridge just visible. Then again, it could be that he felt at home in this kind of environment. He seemed destined for a bigger role at the *Times*, and he was eager to learn about how the paper was run. Perhaps he would one day have a position which allowed him more frequent access to the room.

As they entered, he was sitting at the head of the enormous table, grinning widely. "Ah, Kim and Ian... welcome!"

He gestured to the two smartly dressed visitors sitting at one side of the table.

"This is Tom and Geri from AI-Bel. That's right... Tom and Geri! Here to enjoy a little game of cat and mouse with their favourite clients."

"Nice to meet you," said Kim, moving swiftly to shake hands with the two consultants, who both looked somewhat embarrassed by Jonny's attempts at humour.

"You too," said Geri, "I always enjoy your articles."

"Thanks," replied Kim, smiling at the

compliment. It felt good when people were positive about her work. Life as a writer could be a lonely one, and any feedback normally came via the comments section when her articles were published online.

"Right, let's get into it," said Jonny. "We're here today to talk about the software which AI-Bel have developed, and which we're currently using on the Financial desk. It's a program called AI-Thor. I've invited Kim and Ian along as they are our most senior Sports writers and I'd really like them to hear all about it. I believe Tom and Geri have a presentation for us first. Over to you."

Despite Jonny's introduction, it was clear that Geri was the senior partner in this particular double act, as she rose to her feet and moved to the far end of the table, where a large screen displayed the AI-Bel logo.

Geri had what looked like a small silver pen in her hand. She clicked a button on the top of it and the next slide in the presentation appeared. It showed just two words in bold, black letters:

OUR PURPOSE

"Let me start by explaining why we do what we do." She spoke confidently and clearly. "We believe in the power of information. We believe that we can enrich people's lives by helping to bring them more information more quickly than ever before."

She paused for a moment to let them absorb this, then clicked the button on the device once more and a new slide appeared which showed an image of a smartphone, a tablet, and a laptop.

"In the modern world, people want access to information in many different ways," she continued. "At the *Sydney Times,* you are no longer competing solely with other newspapers. You are competing with a whole range of information sources – social media, dedicated online news sites, bloggers, and so on. Your customers demand that you are able to get them the news that they want, as soon as it happens."

Kim thought back to the start of her day and the way that she had reached for her phone, scanning social media for links to interesting news articles. Geri was right. Everybody wanted news quickly now, and newspapers were struggling to keep pace.

"I'd like to make something very clear from the start, though," Geri went on, "contrary to what some journalists think, we are not doing what we do in an attempt to replace people like you." She fixed her eyes on Ian as she said this, perhaps picking up on his scepticism and nervousness. "In fact, I believe that our software makes room for you to do what you do best: research, investigation, and writing thought-provoking articles."

As the presentation continued, Geri explained to Kim and Ian how the AI-Thor software worked and how it had already been used in preparing some of the output for the Finance section of the paper.

"We take data and feeds from other sources and collate them. The software can identify which aspects of the information it receives are the most important and relevant and can then convert these into a kind of plan for an article. Do you map out or model your articles before you write them?"

"Yes," replied Ian. "It's pretty much the foundation of my process. I use a mind-map to group and link the themes. The writing is actually pretty straightforward after that. Most of the hard work goes into planning."

"That's true of the software, too," said Geri. "When the article plan is converted into plain English, people think it is really impressive, but actually the words and phrases which make up the article are just based on a set of rules."

Kim felt a little alarmed by this. "Hang

on, Geri. You said that the software wasn't intended to replace journalists. From what you just said, it seems like that's exactly what you are doing."

"The difference," replied Geri, "is that the software can only act on the data it receives. It can't investigate to uncover more data, it can't offer opinion and counter-opinion, and of course it doesn't understand the story it is writing."

"So, you're saying that it is kind of dumb?" asked Ian.

Geri smiled. "I wouldn't necessarily choose that word."

"Particularly if you were trying to make a sale," said Jonny drily.

"Let's just say that it has certain limitations," Geri said. "But it is always learning and improving."

Kim noted that the language Geri was using didn't suggest a passive or 'dumb' machine, but one able to solve problems and to increase its capabilities. Regardless, based on what they had been told about its current capabilities, she was feeling a little puzzled.

"So, Geri," she said, "if it can't do what human writers do, what are the advantages of having it?"

"You remember I talked about the different ways people like to receive their news, and the speed they want to receive it?" Geri smiled at Kim. "Well, it all comes down to the volume of information the program can handle and the speed it can respond. I'll let Tom explain."

Her colleague stood, picking up the thread of conversation. "Take your Financial desk, for example," he began. "There are thousands of companies that could be of interest to people who read that section of the paper. There are share prices and financial results to monitor and the software can do all of that, turning the data into meaningful stories."

He went on to explain how the Finance desk could publish much more content than they used to, covering more companies, and providing readers with greater breadth of information. Some of the stories went in the paper but most were digital content for the website.

"Not only that," he continued, "but automated news can be published rapidly. A few years back, there was an earthquake in the USA. The authorities who monitor seismic activity send out real-time data to news agencies and, using this data, one of the local papers was able to publish a story about the earthquake within a few minutes of it happening. All done automatically."

"Sent shockwaves through the industry," Jonny added, grinning again.

"That is pretty impressive," Kim said thoughtfully. "The software, I mean. Not your joke, Jonny." Noting the slightly hurt look on her boss's face, she quickly moved on, asking him, "So what do you want me and Ian to do?"

"It's pretty simple, really," he replied. "I'd like you two to look into how we might be able to use this in Sport. We get so much data on sports results, player performance, movement of players between clubs, and so on. There must be ways we can use it more effectively."

"We can help you with some case studies based on other papers who have used the software for sports stories," added Tom.

"And in most of those case studies, the writers – people like you and Ian – have found themselves working on the more interesting stories. Their time has been freed up by the software," said Geri, directing her attention towards Ian once more.

Kim was impressed with the presentation, and with the explanation of what the software could do. There were clearly some potential benefits for the paper and probably for the writers too. She was happy that Jonny had asked her to get involved in the meeting, and that he trusted her and Ian enough to seek their opinions.

As the meeting concluded, Kim thanked the two visiting consultants, who promised they would be in touch with details of the case studies they had mentioned. Jonny made it clear that he didn't want Kim and Ian to concern themselves with the financial or logistical aspects of bringing in the software. He just wanted an honest assessment of how it could be used. It was notable that he asked 'how' and not 'if'.

"So, what do you think?" Ian asked Kim as the two of them entered the lift.

"It looks pretty good to me," she replied. "I know it's a sales pitch, and I know we should be cautious, but it does seem like the software would be useful to us. How do you feel?"

"I'm not sure. I can see why it would make sense to get more content out, but how good is that content going to be? Our readers don't just want quantity. They want quality as well."

"Maybe we can get some examples of articles produced by this program along with the case studies," Kim said. "It may make you feel a bit better."

"Perhaps," Ian responded, "or perhaps it will make me feel worse. What if the robo-writing is better than mine?"

Kim smiled, registering that her colleague's concerns were rather less serious than earlier. It seemed that maybe he had warmed to the idea.

"Rise of the machines?" she asked.

"Yep. Rise of the machines."

The power of purpose

In Chapter Three, we explored the subject of empathy and the role it can play in product development; how an understanding of what other people might feel can help us to identify with, and create a connection to, them. This connection can help those working in product development to consider some of the human responses which may be triggered by the technology they create and maintain, and the needs and desires of the people their product is intended for.

The meeting with the consultants from AI-Bel in this chapter provides an example of how this awareness can also help to define purpose; a reason for something to be done, and an end goal. During the presentation, Geri shows Kim and her colleagues that AI-Bel is a company which understands why they do what they do, and why their software is required. The presentation begins with an explanation of AI-Bel's vision, and the benefits they can bring to people; in this case through providing readers with news and information. This is not simply a demonstration of a technical product which automatically writes articles. It is a demonstration of how people's lives can be enriched, and they can be empowered, through that information.

This is easy for Kim, Ian and Jonny to relate to their own work as journalists, and to the newspaper's customers. Once Geri has established this connection in their minds, it is much easier to talk about her company's product and how it works. The approach helps to convince Kim of the value of the software. Even Ian, previously nervous and sceptical, comes round to the idea. This isn't a trick on Geri's part. There is nothing underhand going on. She is merely ensuring that the presentation, and the conversation they have, are framed by a shared understanding of purpose.

As we saw in the previous chapter, with the examples of the

Ford Model T and the iPod, a clear purpose can drive the design of great products. Understanding the reasons for doing something requires us to better understand the people we intend to help, and the benefits we aim to bring to them. In product development, starting with a purpose means putting customers first and, by addressing their needs, we are more likely to provide something which they value. If your first conversation about a product is about why people might want it, then this is also your first discussion about quality.

Purpose over process

For those who work in software development, process can sometimes take precedence over purpose. The techniques and tools used in carrying out the work can seem exciting, and there is no shortage of new ideas and skills to learn. The desire to be at the forefront of change, or at the very least to demonstrate awareness and familiarity with current methods, can be a powerful motivator in this field. Adoption of new techniques, training in how to use new tools, and acquisition of knowledge and skills related to new ideas, can become goals in themselves, perhaps inspired by an admirable desire for learning, or possibly a desire to enhance a résumé. In some cases, the new ideas and processes which emerge become causes or movements, with evangelists devoted to sharing the good news about the latest trend.

An example of such a movement in recent years is Continuous Deployment - an approach used to release software to customers on a frequent basis, usually in relatively small packages, with minimal changes.

At an event called 'Velocity 2011', Jon Jenkins discussed Amazon's Continuous Deployment approach as part of a talk which provided insights into some of the company's methods and the associated business benefits. Whilst the audience at the presentation were encouraged to think about business benefits themselves, a statistic from the talk which is often quoted in blogs and articles on Continuous Deployment is perhaps more likely to prompt discussion about how it is done, rather than why.

The revelation that Amazon instigate a release (deployment) every 11.6 seconds, on average, tells us little about the purpose of the approach but because it represents a dramatic shift from models where releases may have occurred in weekly, monthly or sometimes even longer cycles, it is eye-catching for those interested in the process of releasing software.

Continuous Deployment may present an enticing opportunity for individuals to engage in new ways of working, but it does not necessarily follow that it is in the best interests of an organisation or their customers. The capability for rapid and regular changes to a product may provide greater business benefits and customer value in some cases than others, so understanding the purpose of the approach is essential. The potential business benefits of Continuous Deployment - which could include competitive advantage resulting from shorter time to market, the ability to react swiftly to problems or customer feedback, and the potential to avoid spending money building products which people do not want - might not always stack up favourably against the challenges of adjusting to new ways of working and associated costs of establishing the capability (e.g. acquisition of tools and technology; developing and maintaining scripts which automate parts of the process; training, recruitment and retention of people). Meanwhile, the approach may benefit customers, but may also carry risk. Frequent changes to a product may have implications for a customer's experience and their impression of that product (a subject we will return to later).

Defining the purpose of an approach, perhaps with a simple statement similar to the one Geri uses to explain Al-Bel's reasons for doing what they do, can help in weighing up benefits against costs and risks, and in setting out a vision for those involved in making it happen. The process, no matter how exciting it may be, is rarely enough to make a case. When it comes to deciding whether something is worth doing, purpose takes precedence over process.

Designing for people

Away from software development, there are fields where understanding purpose, specifically understanding the intended benefits for people, is crucial. In Urban Design (the design of public space in cities, towns and villages) for example, techniques and principles are adopted which emphasise the needs of inhabitants when planning these environments. In Urban Design, people - and their perception of places - come first. The connection or relationship between those people and places is a key theme. Some of the considerations for an Urban Designer include:

- The suitability of new developments in the context of the existing environment.
- How to help people to 'read' their surroundings by keeping them consistent with other developments, for example by grouping particular types of buildings together, or providing familiar ways of navigating.
- The choices people have in how they move around, the routes and means of transport they can take, and how these affect their surroundings.
- The depth or richness of experiences available to people within the environment.
- How easy it is for people to make use of places for a variety of purposes, for example using parks for sport, recreation, public events, and so on.
- How well people can tailor the space to meet their own needs.
- The human scale of buildings; the relative proportions of elements of the built environment, and how these may affect people.
- 'Future-proofing' of the area to maintain value and enjoyment for people as different factors change the way they live.

There are many more. Consideration will be given to how safe and comfortable a space is, whether it is inclusive and accessible, how appealing it is, and whether the experience of being there is enjoyable. These factors are focused on people because Urban Design brings a human perspective to what may otherwise simply be a functional exercise. By focusing on the real purpose of the spaces, Urban Designers help to create places for people.

Meanwhile, Human-Centered Design (pioneered by the design firm IDEO, and its founder David Kelley) is an approach which advocates a focus on people, the problems they face, and how these problems could be solved. As with Urban Design, this approach helps establish a clear purpose, with people at its heart.

Understanding these people, their needs and their wishes, helps to determine what might be *desirable* to them, but this is just one of three lenses applied in Human-Centered Design when assessing the suitability of a potential solution. The other two lenses are used to consider whether that solution is technically *feasible* and economically *viable*.

Some of the methods suggested as part of the approach include interviews with the individuals or groups affected, and immersion in their lives; spending time with them to observe the way they go about things, the tasks they carry out, and some of the problems they face. Designers are also encouraged to pay attention to feelings and instincts they may have whilst carrying out their work; feelings which might result from previous experiences and the knowledge they have built up, or from their human responses to the people they are working with. Empathy is a strong theme in Human-Centered Design, because a truly human-centred approach requires deep connection with the people the solutions are intended to help.

The techniques used in Human-Centered Design, and the consideration given to human connection by Urban Designers, demonstrate the importance of purpose in these domains, and the emphasis on people, their needs and their wishes, in defining that purpose. This focus influences not only the work of the designers but inevitably the tasks and activities which follow in developing and maintaining the places and solutions. Benefits for, and connections with, humans are the true measure of success.

As we have seen in the earlier sections of the book, the purpose of software and other technology has not always been given the same consideration. There has been a disconnect between products, the people who develop them, and the people they are intended for. Some of the cultural changes, and the practices discussed, following Chapter Two are intended to bridge this gap. There may now be greater awareness of the need for empathy, and an increased desire to deliver value to customers, but can more be learned from other domains?

Perhaps the thought which Urban Designers give to the different aspects which affect the human connection with the places they shape can teach us something about how to understand the connection between people and technology. Meanwhile, there may be lessons from Human-Centered Design in how to put people, rather than processes, at the centre of our thinking, and how to view products from their perspective. In doing so, purpose will become clearer, and we will perhaps be better positioned to understand what quality means to our customers.

Three Dimensions of Quality

So far, we have seen that quality can be a complex subject, not least for those who develop software and other technology.

This is a significant challenge when the work brings together different people, each with their own skills, experiences, biases and opinions, shaping individual notions of quality and potentially leading to different assumptions about what might represent quality to someone else.

We have seen how empathy and a clear sense of purpose can help to bring the feelings, needs and desires of prospective customers into product development; we have looked at some of the lessons that could be learned from other fields, where great care is taken to put humans at the centre of what they do.

As we bring these factors and observations together, we can see that a more human-centred view of quality in technology could help overcome some of the challenges we have discussed, encouraging empathy, and clarifying the purpose of products. In short, such a model could help in understanding the complex relationship between people and technology.

In this section I will introduce the 'Three Dimensions of Quality' model; a simple representation of some of the many factors which can affect the impression a person forms of a product. The model is influenced by the human focus in the principles and techniques of Urban Design and Human-Centered Design, but also by the many quality characteristics or quality criteria which are used in software development (some sources of these can be found in the 'References and Further Reading' section at the end of the book).

Three Dimensions of Quality

The dimensions and aspects of quality are intended to be considered from a human perspective; from the point of view of the customer. We therefore start at the centre of the model, with customer perception. Throughout this book, we will explore the layers of the model using examples, many of which are based on Kim's experiences. In these examples, we can think of Kim as a persona; a representation of a hypothetical potential customer, or a person a product is intended to help. The use of personas in product development can help to understand the needs of real people, and the different ways they may use a product. In our story, it is often Kim's perception which is influenced by the dimensions and quality aspects but when using the model, a customer could be any person whose perception of a product matters.

Moving out from the centre, we reach the three dimensions affecting the relationship between person and product:

DESIRABLE: The extent to which our needs and wishes are fulfilled. Are we getting what we want? Is our experience a positive one?

DEPENDABLE: The extent to which we trust and feel that we can rely on a product. Do we feel safe and protected? Is it there when we need it?

DURABLE: The extent to which a product's value to us endures. If the product changes, or our needs and desires change; do they still align?

These three Ds can be significant factors in many relationships, including those between a person and a product. Although they might not all be significant for the relationship between every person and every product, each can be critical in certain circumstances.

Each of the dimensions is also the nucleus of a collection of quality aspects; some of the many factors which can influence a person's impression of a product. As we proceed, we will explore these aspects in more detail.

Notes on the model

Before we look further into the quality aspects, there are some important points to note. Firstly, the model is not intended as a standard or a checklist. The three dimensions and the quality aspects should not be interpreted as a comprehensive, static view of quality. Based on the earlier description of quality as subjective and variable, any attempt to provide such a definitive view would be futile. The quality aspects we will cover offer a perspective on factors which might be important to one or more people using a particular product at a given time. Depending on the context, each of us could have a different view on which aspects matter to us, perhaps including factors not mentioned here.

Instead, the model is intended to help individuals, teams and organisations to think about quality from a human perspective and to discuss which aspects may be of particular significance in their context.

It should also be noted that the quality aspects may contribute to a person's perception of more than one of the dimensions. For the purposes of the model they are grouped with, but not necessarily unique to, the dimensions. Depending on the product and the person using it, the aspects might be considered more relevant to one of the other dimensions.

Finally, the language used in the model - the words adopted for the different dimensions and aspects - are intended to be simple and understandable; the kind of words that might be used by the people who use technology, and not just the people who create or maintain it[1].

---

[1] Readers who work in the development of technology might be familiar with quality criteria or quality characteristics expressed as 'ities' (words like Scalability, Testability and Portability) and as they read on they may wonder where the 'ities' have gone. Whilst some of the quality aspects are similar to those in other lists, some of the language used here might seem a little strange. It is worth remembering that for those outside this field, the 'ities' themselves might seem like a strange language.

This is in no way intended to disparage the lists of quality criteria or quality characteristics which already exist. If technology is not testable, scalable or portable, for example, this may well have a profound effect on the product and the people who use it, and whilst some of these

The Three Dimensions of Quality model encourages us to consider quality from a human perspective, shifting the focus to the customer and their perception of the product. What does quality mean to them? What matters to them? As we will see, there are many aspects which could play a part in answering these questions.

---

more technical criteria are not covered in these chapters, their importance is not underestimated. I see no reason why product quality cannot be considered from a technical and a human perspective.

Chapter Five: Beautiful sites

During the afternoon, the office had emptied significantly. Kim's colleagues had clearly decided to get out and about to work on some of the stories they had discussed that morning. It was quiet and there were some empty desks near the windows, offering views to the east across the city, so Kim had decided to stick around a little longer. As she looked up, she could see that the skies were darkening. The warm, sunny day was about to give way to a stormy evening. She had been absorbed in her work for a couple of hours and had made some good progress. Perhaps if she left now, she might just miss the rain.

She packed up her things and made her way downstairs. As she was about to leave the building through the huge glass doors, Jonny spotted her. He was in the seating area outside the lobby café where she had met Ian earlier that afternoon.

He waved, got up from his seat, and walked over to her. "Thanks for your help with the AI-Bel meeting."

"No problem," Kim replied. "It was pretty interesting, actually."

"It doesn't bother you, then?"

"What? The idea of automated writing?"

Jonny nodded.

"I guess it depends," said Kim. "It's all about how and when we make use of it, and how well written the content is. I suppose it comes back to our readers. If we are providing them with more content and the stories are well written then that has to be a good thing, doesn't it?"

Jonny smiled. He wasn't giving much away.

Their conversation came to an end as Ken Price, the Editor of the *Times*, emerged from the lifts and started across the lobby. Jonny wished Kim a good evening and walked over to Ken. As Kim went outside, she glanced back and saw the two men talking, Jonny's arm outstretched as if gesturing in her direction.

She didn't escape the rain.

As she walked towards her bus stop, a downpour began. Kim looked in her bag and realised that her umbrella was back at home. This was a problem, partly because it meant there was little chance of avoiding a drenching, but more importantly because she had no means of defence against the umbrellas which other people were carrying and which they seemed intent on poking into her eyes.

Her bus was already at the stop. She was a good distance away when she spotted it so she ran towards it, gesturing at the driver in the hope that he would wait for her. Fortunately for Kim, this driver was more sympathetic than the one she had spoken to that morning. He waited and offered a smile as she stepped onto the vehicle, wet from the rain and slightly out of breath from her short run.

"Thank you!" she said as she searched for her travel card.

"No worries," replied the driver. "I didn't want to leave you behind in this weather. Just take a seat and find your card. No rush."

Kim did as he suggested and took a few seconds to compose herself. She located the card and when the bus stopped at some lights she tapped it on the reader. No problems this time. A pinging sound and the trip registered right away. It did, however, remind her that she needed to sort out the morning's journey. What had happened, given that she hadn't been able to register the end of the trip?

She pulled her tablet from her bag and opened up the public transport website. There was a section dedicated to travel cards, with some information on the different types, fares, and so on. There was also a list of 'Frequently Asked Questions' and, sure enough, this included some information on what would happen in the event of a journey not being completed (at least as far as the machine and ticket were concerned – it seemed to Kim that for the person involved all journeys were completed one way or another). Apparently, there was a maximum fare which would be applied in this case, and the journey would not count towards the weekly bonus – a system which allowed for cheap travel after a certain number of journeys had been made in a week.

Kim logged in to check whether this had happened for her trip that morning. The page for her account details had a picture of a travel card with her name on it. When she clicked on the picture, the image of the card changed to show the balance remaining and a list of recent trips. There was the morning's bus ride and it had indeed been registered as a 'Max Fare' trip, although the charge looked to be the same as what she normally paid for her journey to work. It hadn't cost her anything extra but Kim wanted to let them know that there had been a problem with the machine so she had been unable to tap off through no fault of her own. Besides anything else, she wanted to register the journey towards the weekly bonus.

Under the picture of her travel card on the website, there was a short message which said:

Contact us if something doesn't look right

The bit that was underlined linked to another page, where Kim's card details were again displayed and there was a box where she could enter a message. She typed an explanation of what had happened earlier that day and clicked on the button to send her message. It was all very quick and simple to use, unlike the OzTelia website which she had been struggling with earlier.

As she was putting the tablet away she spotted a notification alert on the screen of her phone, which was protruding from a side pocket of her bag. There was a message from Paul in London:

Hi, got your email. I'll see what I can find out about the chat with Chloe

It would be early morning in the UK. The time of the message showed that it had come through a few minutes earlier, whilst Kim was on the tablet. She sent a reply:

Thanks! Let me know if I need to do anything to prepare

There was a short delay, then another message appeared:

It will be pretty informal I think but maybe have a look around our website for a bit of background info

This was something she had intended to do anyway. She had hoped Paul might be able to shed a little light on the kind of role which might be available at the magazine. If he knew, he wasn't letting on, or perhaps she was just being too subtle in her inquiries. It didn't really matter.

She could ask Chloe directly about what sort of work she had in mind when they spoke. In the meantime, an evening spent poking around the *Two Halves* website would be interesting. If nothing else, there were certain to be some good stories to read.

Kim could see why *Two Halves* was such a successful venture. The website was excellent. There was a news stream, with video reports as well as written articles, and detailed coverage of football activity around the world. An interactive map allowed website visitors to focus on countries or regions which interested them, and to follow matches with real-time updates on scores and incidents. The breadth of coverage was incredible. Updates weren't limited to high-profile matches in England, Spain, or the other major European leagues. If there was a professional football match going on anywhere in the world, some level of reporting and analysis was provided.

A prominent section on the site was called 'Community' and included lively forums, which Kim browsed briefly, noticing that despite this being a website devoted to football, the sport didn't feature in some of the discussions. Recent subjects included other sports, politics, films and television series. In one thread, there was a heated debate about a fictional children's television character. Obviously some of the contributors had a little too much time on their hands. The forums did indeed seem to be a community, with moderators from within the group who weeded out anything which was unsuitable for the pages and who had the power to block people from the site.

There was much more content besides – in fact it seemed that, despite the more targeted subject matter, there was more here than on the website for the *Times* – and the whole site had a feeling of fun and vibrancy. Kim had been rather naïve in her belief that this magazine was less prestigious than the paper. She was eager to see more and so paid for an annual digital subscription, which gave her access to a tablet version of the magazine. This allowed her to select geographical areas and leagues which she was interested in and, based on these choices, provided a selection of in-depth articles from the feature writers. As she had suspected, the writing was excellent, and the passion for the sport shone through in everything she read.

Feeling energised by the experience, Kim searched for more information on some of the writers who were mentioned on the *Two Halves* site. Several of them had accounts on the social media sites she used, and she noted that many of them had more followers than her. Clearly, the magazine provided a good platform for journalists to develop their reach and reputation. The idea of joining them was becoming increasingly appealing.

As she settled into bed that night, Kim picked up her phone and continued looking through the online activity from the magazine's writers but she remembered the vow she had made earlier. This was supposed to be a time for reading her book, not looking at social media. A time to relax the mind and wind down after a busy day. She looked over at the book on her bedside table, then back to the glowing screen. Maybe just a few more minutes.

Desirable quality

In the Three Dimensions of Quality model, the word 'desirable' is used not only as a measure of attractiveness to the human senses, but also of how much a person may wish for something. It is worth noting that a product may seem desirable before use but may become less so during use, and vice versa. This section covers fourteen different aspects of quality which relate to a product being desirable.

As Kim explores the *Two Halves* website, she notices many aspects which might make it desirable to her and to others. Kim is actively researching the site as much as its content, so may be paying more attention than usual to what it offers and how it works. She enjoys the experience, and is conscious of what it is that she likes about it. When she pays for a subscription, this is partly driven by the forthcoming interview and a need to familiarise herself with the site, but it is also down to the positive impression she forms as she investigates the content.

Often when we use technology, we are not so attuned to the way it works or how it is helping us. We simply want to get on with whatever we are doing. If using technology feels **EFFORTLESS** we may not notice but if the opposite is true and we are required to stop what we are doing to figure out how to use something, we almost certainly will.

If technology fits seamlessly into our lives, we can concentrate on performing the tasks and activities which it supports. If its behaviour or appearance presents us with problems - unwanted distractions or hurdles to overcome - then our attention has to shift, which can be frustrating. To this end, it is also important that a product is **UNINTRUSIVE**. You may recall from the first chapter Kim's annoyance at the advert which redirected her to another website as she browsed a news site. Active 'pop ups' - for example a window asking us to install an upgrade, or restart a machine - can be another source of irritation, interrupting the flow of a process and requiring us to divert our attention elsewhere.

The way a product is designed, its behaviour, and how easy it is to learn and operate, are all related to how **USABLE** it is. Kim navigates the travel card website with ease and this allows her to focus on the task in hand. It is an **INTUITIVE** site where Kim can quickly find what she needs and complete tasks with little difficulty. This may simply mean that the website is **CONSISTENT** with other websites. Links and information can be found in similar places, and the behaviour may be familiar (for example, the underlined text represents a link to another area of the site, or another site entirely). To be consistent, the appearance and behaviour must also be harmonious across the site. It must be consistent with itself as much as with other similar products.

From a customer's perspective, the usability of a system or application may also extend into how easy it is to install or setup and, if necessary, to remove or 'uninstall' it. These are distinct stages of the usage of a product, but they do relate to ease of use, and they can certainly affect our impression of that product. Many consumers are accustomed to applications which are simple to download and install on mobile devices. This sets a benchmark by which other products may well be judged, and laborious installation processes are not a positive first step in the relationship between human and technology. When software is pre-installed on devices this may remove potential installation problems for a customer but, if that software is not wanted, there might be other problems. If, for example, pre-installed software is intrusive, providing frequent, uninvited requests to 'upgrade' the product, this may well cause frustration and annoyance. This can be compounded if the software is not easy to remove.

Also related to usability is the question of how **INCLUSIVE** a product is; whether the different needs of potential customers have been considered in the design and the means of operation. For example, some people are unable to operate a computer's mouse and may need keyboard controls as an alternative. Others have reduced vision and make use of a screen reader - software which converts text and other content to speech and which is dependent on the use of text alternatives to images, and labels to identify the different elements (buttons, menus, text fields, etc.) of websites and applications. Many websites include audio as well as visual elements. For example, the *Two Halves* website which Kim explores contains video news items. Providing captions or text transcripts for this kind of content makes it more inclusive for people who cannot hear the audio elements.

There are many other examples of how people's diverse needs and abilities can affect their experiences with technology. People who are colour-blind may have difficulty with the contrast of particular coloured text and backgrounds. Others may find too much choice or content distracts them from concentrating on a task. Some people may simply not be comfortable or familiar with using technology, including websites and applications.

The opinions, experiences and biases which we discussed after Chapter Two will certainly play a part in whether, or how far, designers and developers consider these diverse needs. However, if a product is created with awareness of the many ways it might be used, and if consideration is given by the people responsible for its design and development to all those who might need to use it, it is far more likely to be an inclusive product.

Whilst many countries have legislation relating to discrimination in the provision of goods and services[2], there are other compelling reasons to make products more inclusive, including wider benefits relating to how usable a product is. For example, a clear layout designed with people who are less comfortable with technology in mind may also be considered a better design by others, despite not sharing those same limitations. Voice recognition features, which help those who are unable to use a keyboard, are now common in mobile device and computer operating systems, and in applications such as Google Maps. Inclusive products can have benefits for all the people who use them.

Two more quality aspects related to the 'desirable' dimension are how **USEFUL** and **ENJOYABLE** a product is. Depending on the purpose of the product, it might need to fulfil both requirements. In the case of the travel card website, Kim is looking to complete a rather mundane task, but one which is important to her. By helping her to do so, the site is useful. Visitors to the *Two Halves* website, meanwhile, might be looking for more entertainment and something more stimulating. The articles, forums and quizzes available on the site may well provide them with this.

There are other examples of products where customers are likely to be concerned with one of these criteria more than the other.

Customers downloading a game to play on their phone would almost certainly feel disappointed if the game was not enjoyable. It would not need to provide any great practical

---

[2]   An   excellent   summary   of   such   legislation   can   be   found   here: http://webaim.org/articles/laws/world/

purpose; it could be entirely frivolous. Meanwhile, a software package for accounting would certainly need to be useful to people who kept financial records or tracked income and outgoings. If the same package didn't provide them with a sense of joy or pleasure this might not be a surprise, or a problem, for them. The same could apply to a website or application used annually by a customer to renew an insurance policy, or a utility for printing from a mobile device.

In other cases, both aspects might be important to customers. The market for sport- and fitness-related devices and applications demonstrates how products can be useful and enjoyable. The primary purpose of these products is to assist people in setting goals related to their health and well-being and in tracking progress towards these goals. This could be achieved through some basic and functional technology - simple pedometers, for example, which count the number of steps someone takes in a day. By bringing a 'gaming' element into the devices, for example integrating step counts with an app which allows people to 'virtually walk' in famous locations or along well-known routes, the experience is enhanced.

Nintendo's Wii Fit, which launched in 2007, was a product which perhaps tipped the balance between the two criteria towards enjoyment, yet it was extremely useful for many people too, allowing them to track changes in their weight and posture over time whilst they played the different fitness-related games on offer.

In part, the impression which Kim forms of the *Two Halves* website is determined by how **RICH** in features it is. Kim notices this during a relatively brief visit to a website, but richness can become more important when we start to use a product more extensively. In the case of the word-processing application I am using to write this book, I have recently discovered new (to me at least) features which have been useful. This is probably because I am using the application more regularly than before and the nature of the work requires me to do some things differently.

Another example which has helped me in my work on the

book is a note-taking app, which allows me to save links to web pages, attach files and voice memos, take photos, make sketches of diagrams, and much more. The app is rich in features which are valuable to me.

Alongside, and related to, the features which the note-taking app possesses is another highly useful aspect. The app is **COMPATIBLE** with different devices. Notes can be saved on a phone or tablet and are then 'synced' so that they are available on a laptop or desktop computer that has the same application installed. It is also compatible with other applications, enabling attachment of different types of files to notes.

Compatibility between devices, systems and applications can increase their usefulness, providing benefits which might not be possible when they are used in isolation. Digital cameras were popular before smartphones and the rise of the social media giants but once we were able to take photos anywhere at any time, using social media apps and websites to share photos with groups of friends or followers, and observing their responses and comments, the combination of technologies was greater than the sum of its parts.

With greater richness in many of the products we use, and expanding integration of technology in our lives, personalisation has become a feature of some of those products. Increasingly, our experiences can be **PERSONALISED**, either directly - by us - or indirectly - by logic and algorithms which respond to our actions and behaviour.

When Kim purchases a subscription to *Two Halves* magazine, she benefits from the ability to personalise the application. Appropriate content is provided according to the subjects she selects; the virtual magazine becomes a magazine just for Kim.

When personalisation is within our control, for example in the way we configure the appearance of a system's interface, or the privacy settings we select for an application, the extent to which it can be adjusted may be extremely important to us. The ability to change how a product looks or operates, and the extent to which information about how, when and where we use a product is provided to others, gives us choice.

Perhaps the most familiar examples of this choice are in the operating systems installed on our mobile devices and computers. They are highly configurable, perhaps to the extent that the choices can be a little bewildering at times. Even relatively simple smartphone operating systems include options relating to Bluetooth and WiFi connections, battery usage, privacy, accessibility, sounds, appearance of lock screens and home screens, groupings of apps, screen brightness, timings for 'auto-lock', text size, 'autofill' of fields, and so on. This is before we even begin to look through the options for each of the pre-installed applications which may offer choices related to notifications, location services, alerts, call forwarding, choice of search engine, read receipts, sorting, additional layers of protection, and many, many more. It would be easy to forget that changing nothing in the default settings is also a choice. The way a device is initially configured could be significant.

When personalisation is somewhat outside our control, we will probably be concerned with how **RELEVANT** it is. Many of us are familiar with content provided to us based on earlier interactions; for example, the television shows which a media streaming service suggests might be of interest to us based on previous viewing, or the prospective contacts suggested to us by a social media app based on our existing contacts. If we know that our online behaviour is monitored and our choices and actions are tracked, in return we might demand that our experiences are tailored. If this is done well, it may be easier to understand why our behaviour is monitored in this way.

Some personalisation can be unwelcome or confusing. In the case of retargeting - the use of advertising related to products which we have previously shown an interest in - it can seem intrusive or, perhaps, illogical. If, for example, I purchase a new television through the website of an electronics retailer, it is unlikely that I will want to buy another one in the near future, yet I may well be bombarded with adverts for televisions on other websites for weeks to come.

Many of these factors relate to how products operate. While these can affect how much a person may wish to own or use a product, desirability can also be driven by the appearance of a product and how visually **APPEALING** it is. This might apply to the physical design of a device - for example, a thin, sleek laptop with carefully contrasting surfaces may be sold on the basis of its external design as much as on its technical capabilities - or it may be a factor in software or website design.

Websites are a good example of how visual appeal can contribute to the impression formed of products and organisations. The sites can be a 'shop window', drawing customers in, or perhaps encouraging them to move on somewhere else, so their appearance can matter. The design of websites therefore includes consideration of many factors, not only related to ease of use, but also to the aesthetics of the site. The layout, proportions of the various elements, colour schemes, textures and typefaces, use of images and other content, can all play a part in how a site looks and in the reaction it inspires.

For some, the perception of quality may be influenced by how **NOVEL** a product is. This certainly does not apply to everybody, but it may in the case of early adopters, who value being among the first to gain access to a product.

When people queue for hours, or even days, outside the Apple store to buy the latest iPhone model, they are not just paying for a phone but also the opportunity to break new ground, to try something innovative, or simply to be the first among their social circle to own the new release. The differences between the models may not seem significant to others - at least not significant enough that they need to get their hands on the latest device quickly - but for the people who do care about this, the novelty factor matters.

Novelty does not necessarily mean that a product has to be new to a market. Weeks, months and even years after the launch of the original iPhone in 2007, many more people may have experienced a sense of excitement as they tried the device for the first time. Even for those who wouldn't consider themselves to be early adopters, there may still be great pleasure to be derived from the freshness of a product which is new to them.

This is a wide-ranging subject and there are many more factors which could play a part; some of these are covered in the following sections, about the criteria which can make products Dependable and Durable. Before that, however, here is a recap of the quality aspects covered in this section:

Desirable
appealing compatible consistent effortless enjoyable inclusive intuitive novel personalised relevant rich usable useful unintrusive

Chapter Six: Successful connections

Thursday was always a busy day. As they headed towards the deadline for the weekend's feature articles there was lots of activity. Jonny liked to have a preliminary layout for the Sunday sports section by Friday afternoon so the feature content needed to be ready by the end of Thursday. Sometimes, if an article was going through a lot of rework, 'the end of Thursday' could be late in the evening. Kim wanted to make sure that this was not the case today. She needed to be home and ready for the call with Chloe.

Unfortunately, events were conspiring against her. Kim had been forced to make some changes to her feature story – a detailed look at the ongoing exodus of Australian rugby international players to European clubs, and the implications for the national side. This was an article which she had been working on for the last two weeks and it had been more or less ready to go for a couple of days now.

Just this morning, however, a story had broken about a high-profile player who had signed for a French club and would now be likely to miss the next World Cup due to rules about selection of players from outside Australia. This would be great in terms of driving interest in Kim's story (Ian often said that she had a sixth sense - writing stories which seemed to tie in with events in the lead-up to publishing) but it also meant that this breaking news had to be factored in to the article.

She had worked the new angle into the story, and even managed to have a brief chat with the player involved, thanks to a contact at his current club. He hadn't been prepared to go on the record about his motivation for moving but she had picked up some general points about the benefits of playing overseas which had helped in putting some context around the piece.

Once the changes were made, Kim needed to upload the article using the newspaper's editing system. All of the writers had access to a web page where they could enter the text of the article, and add some information about it. These bits of information, referred to as 'tags', could include keywords about the subject (for example, this article would be tagged with 'Rugby' and with the names of players mentioned) and also details of the newspaper section, the writer, and so on. All of this was used to create searchable content on the website and mobile apps so that potential readers would be able to find it.

In theory, articles could be written in the editing page itself, saved, and then reopened for further work later. None of the writers Kim knew felt comfortable doing this – like her, they preferred to use a separate word processor package and then copy and paste the finished articles into the required place on the web page when they needed to submit them to the editors.

The trouble was that the journalists didn't really trust the editing page. It didn't happen often but there had been instances of writers losing changes which they had made on the page, even after they had saved them. Nobody had been able to explain why things sometimes seemed to go missing and Kim had heard one of the IT guys who worked on the page saying that it was probably just that the writers hadn't saved their changes properly. "User error," he had said. What was indisputable was that sometimes the page wasn't always available. Kim had seen the message about the page being unavailable often enough to remember the error number (503) that always went with the message. Even if the page was available and she didn't see this message, it could sometimes take far too long to get a response when submitting a piece. She was often left wondering whether her work had been sent through properly and quite often she had to double-check with the editing staff in person.

These kinds of problems always seemed to happen at the worst possible times, when all the writers were trying to work on their articles. This was one such time. Kim wanted to get the new version of her piece to Jonny so that he could make any final tweaks and pass it over to the design team, but the page wouldn't open.

"The submission page is down again," she said to Ian, who was sitting at the desk opposite.

"Let me guess… our friend 503 again? It must be one of those 'difficult' days," he replied.

"Seems like a difficult day is any day

ending in the letter 'y'," observed Kim. "It's completely useless. I can't do anything."

"I thought they were going to do something to improve it after last week. Looks like you'll have to do it the old-fashioned way again," Ian said. "Just email it to Jonny."

This was the only option, but it meant that Kim would have to go back and add the tags later. Also, Jonny would be annoyed if everybody ended up emailing him their work like they had last Thursday. It made the whole process of reviewing and formatting more laborious.

"OK. Done," she said as she hit the 'send' button on the email. "I'm out of here. I'll speak to you tomorrow."

"Sure, have a good evening," replied Ian distractedly. It seemed like he still had some way to go to get his article finished.

Kim grabbed her things and headed out. She felt a little guilty that she hadn't told Ian about the interview with Chloe but she didn't really want to mention it until she knew whether there was a chance of it leading somewhere.

Unexpectedly, Kim started to feel nervous as the time for the interview approached. The prospect of working for *Two Halves* seemed increasingly appealing after looking into their website and the various features and articles. She had also searched for some background information about Chloe and discovered someone who was, it seemed, admired and respected. As the first female editor of a major sports publication in the UK, she had broken a glass ceiling. Women were still massively under-represented in sports journalism but Chloe's progress had motivated others to follow in her footsteps, judging by the discussions in some of the online forums for journalists. Chloe had also picked up a number of prestigious awards during her career. It seemed she would be a source of inspiration and someone to learn from.

For these reasons, along with a sense of professional pride, Kim was keen to make a good impression. The enthusiasm which Chloe had demonstrated in their interactions so far gave her a belief that the magazine wanted to bring her on board. She was confident in her own work, but she knew that she must also take care to be prepared. Her experience as a journalist had taught her about the importance of planning.

With this in mind, Kim had arranged a quick call with Paul to make sure everything was working OK with the new video messaging account she was setting up. Although she used the same application frequently to make video calls to interview people, and to discuss stories with colleagues, this was always on her work laptop, using an account which the *Times* had set up for her. Tonight, she had decided to install a personal account for the service on her tablet.

There wasn't a great deal of time before the call with Chloe so Kim wanted to try the new account and the app as soon as possible, which meant bypassing any unnecessary parts of the setup process. She paused as she saw the links to the company's terms and conditions, and their privacy policy. This was important, of course, but she didn't really have time to read through the pages of legal terms. How bad could they be? After all, millions of people around the world used this software. She decided to move on to the rest of the process and was soon logged in, using her new account.

She located Paul in the directory and gave him a call. After a couple of rings, the call seemed to connect, and a few seconds later a distorted image of his face appeared. It looked as though he was trying to say something but there was no sound coming from the tablet's speakers.

"Hi Paul, can you hear me?" Kim asked.

There was no response. She gave it a few more seconds and then tried again, a bit more urgently this time. "Paul?"

Again, no response. The picture of Paul now seemed to have frozen and the nervous feeling in Kim's stomach was becoming increasingly intense.

Suddenly, the screen went black and the tablet emitted a low beep, indicating that the connection had been lost. Kim put her hands to her head. Why was this happening now? She was just about to try calling Paul again when the tablet lit up once more and the ring for an incoming call sounded. Paul had got there first.

She quickly pressed the green button on the screen to answer the call.

"Hi, Kim. Can you hear me OK?"

Kim breathed a sigh of relief. His voice was clear and the picture of him was crisp. She could see him properly now and she noticed that he was framed by a background of green hills and blue sky.

"Yes! Loud and clear now," she replied. "I was a bit worried then. Could you hear me before?"

"I could, but you sounded a bit like a robot. It was pretty funny, actually."

Kim smiled. "Yeah, you looked kind of like a Picasso painting," she said. "Eyes and ears in all the wrong places."

"An improvement, I guess?" Paul grinned

back at her.

"You said it. No, seriously, it is good to see you. Where are you? Looks like you're out for a walk in the country."

"I wish," he replied. "I'm working. Hang on, I'll show you."

He turned the camera round to reveal a football training ground. There was a practice match in progress and she could hear the shouts of the players.

"Cheltenham," he said. "They've got a big cup match at the weekend so I'm going to interview some of the players and staff after training."

"It looks beautiful there," Kim replied.

"Yeah, it might look that way but it's absolutely freezing standing here. Can't wait to get in for a cup of tea. Anyway, more importantly, are you all set for 'the chat'?" He emphasised the words for dramatic effect.

"Ha, yes I think so. You got any inside information for me?"

"Sorry, can't help… I'm not even sure what she has in mind for you. Maybe something on the league over there, or maybe the Asian leagues. Might involve some travel if you're lucky."

"OK, no worries," said Kim. "I guess I'll find out soon enough."

The clock at the top of the screen

showed that it was almost time to speak to Chloe.

"It's almost nine here," she continued. "I'd better get off now but I'll let you know how it goes."

"No problem," replied her friend. "Good luck! Not that you'll need it. You'll be fine. See you soon!"

"Thanks, Paul. See you."

She disconnected the call. Hopefully the one with Chloe would be as smooth as that, and she wouldn't sound like a robot again. A good, clear connection would allow her to focus on the conversation.

At nine o'clock, Kim located Chloe in the list of contacts, took a deep breath, and started the video call. After a few seconds, Chloe answered.

"Hi there, Kim, it's great to talk at last."

Thankfully the picture and sound seemed to be fine. Chloe was sitting in what looked like a large meeting room. On the wall behind her, Kim could see framed posters which showed front covers of various editions of Two Halves.

"Hi Chloe, yes, it's taken a while, hasn't it? How are you?"

"Very well, thanks. Busy, of course. We're a couple of weeks out from the next print edition but the digital channels keep me on my toes."

"I can imagine. I've been looking round the website. It's fantastic – so much content – but it must mean that you're always working hard there."

"We certainly are. I'm lucky to have a good group of editors working with me. It really takes the pressure off." There was a brief pause, then Chloe continued. "I have lots I'd like to discuss with you, Kim, but before I get started, is there anything you wanted to ask me? I know we've exchanged a couple of emails but I haven't really told you much about what we do or how we do it."

"To be honest, I have lots of questions for you." Kim smiled and showed Chloe the pages of her notebook where she had jotted down a long list of things to talk about. "If it's OK with you I'd rather just ask things as we go along… maybe if we've missed anything, I can come back to it at the end."

"Of course! I'm glad you came prepared."

"There is one thing I probably should ask upfront. What sort of role did you have in mind for me? I just want to make sure that I understand the context for the conversation."

"Well, I'm glad you mentioned the website because that's something I specifically wanted to talk to you about.

I know you've been working closely with your digital team there at the *Times* – a fine paper, by the way – and I wondered if you might be interested in a role more focused in that area?"

"On the digital side of things? Well, yes, I mean I've really enjoyed the work I've done on the website and I'm excited by the way we can get news and content to readers so quickly now. I love the creative side, too – the ways we can use different types of media to add depth." Kim thought for a second, then added, "I love writing too, though. First and foremost, I'm a writer, and nothing matches the feeling of finding a really good story, investigating and researching, and putting something out which I'm proud of."

Kim could see that Chloe was nodding as she said all this.

"I totally understand that. In fact, I'm very much the same. I started out as a writer and I still enjoy the buzz of working on a big story. I have lots of other responsibilities now but all of our editors, including me, write for the magazine. One of the advantages of working at a magazine is that our print cycles are much longer. We can really devote some time to feature articles. As long as we balance this with the need for more of the on-demand stuff, there is time to write. But coming back to your question, I really need to find someone to come in as a digital editor, initially as a deputy to Grant - our current Digital Editor - but then taking on a bigger role. We're planning a much greater global presence, with dedicated content in different regions. We will need people who can run those regional desks but I want those people to spend time operating with our team here first. I can guarantee that there would be plenty of freedom for writing, but it would also be an opportunity to develop editing skills and to make use of some of the wonderful technology at our disposal."

"Wow," replied Kim, "it sounds really exciting."

"It will be. The sport is growing all over the world and we want to grow with it."

"Do you mind if I ask where the role would be based?"

"Not at all… please ask anything you like. I'd much prefer to have an open conversation. It would be in our new offices in Manchester. We've moved most of our team up to the Media City in Salford. There would be plenty of scope for travel, though. We need stories from all over the UK and Europe, and increasingly we need people to travel further afield."

Kim had vaguely considered that working in the UK might be an option but had thought it far more likely that she would be talking about work she could do from Sydney, making use of her knowledge of the Australian game and her local contacts.

Chloe seemed to read her thoughts. "I realise it would be a big change for you and I wouldn't want you to feel uncomfortable with anything but let's talk some more and see how you feel. If we get to the stage where we both agree we want to work together, the rest will work itself out. First of all, I'd like to find out a bit more about your ideas and what motivates you."

They talked for a long time. It turned out that *Two Halves* was already making use of the AI-Thor software which Kim had been tasked with evaluating. In discussing this they established common ground; some shared concerns but a mutual feeling of positivity for the future of their profession. They discussed how the news business had changed over the last decade and how the newspapers were now competing with social media as much as with each other. Chloe was keen to talk about how they could make better use of social media themselves, and Kim felt comfortable enough to share some of her concerns about moving into writing about a single sport, albeit the most popular sport in the world.

By the end of the call they had built a strong rapport and it seemed that things had gone well for both parties. Chloe promised that she would be in touch but explained that it might take a couple of weeks to work through some of the organisational changes they were making. For Kim, there was an exhilarating feeling, the prospect of an exciting new chapter in her life. She had soon forgotten her earlier concerns about the quality of the call. It had been a successful connection in every respect.

Dependable quality

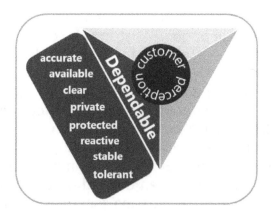

In the Three Dimensions of Quality model the word 'dependable' is used as a measure of the trust a person has in a product, or how reliable they feel it is. This section focuses on eight aspects of a product's dependability.

Technology has brought new ways of working, communicating, buying goods, arranging services, and much more besides. These activities can be performed on computers and other devices in our homes, and mobile devices when outside our homes. Meanwhile, as tasks and activities become more reliant on technology, other options become more scarce. Many organisations are seeking to reduce costs by closing or scaling down expensive physical locations and operations (for example stores, branches and call centres), and encouraging greater use of digital channels. Dependency on those channels is increasing.

If somebody's ability to use other means for important tasks is restricted, the benefits of technology can be profound. For example, alternative methods might require physical access at locations which are difficult to reach for people with reduced mobility, or may rely on mediums which cannot be easily interpreted by people with visual or hearing impairments. In some circumstances, websites, applications, devices, and other technology are essential to fulfilling basic human needs or carrying out compulsory tasks. This becomes more than a question of whether someone might want to use technology; they may have little option. What may be convenient for some people might be essential for others. In this context, dependable technology is essential.

Kim's experiences with the newspaper's editing page, and with the video call software she uses, provide some examples of ways in which we can form an impression of how dependable technology is. Trust is a key word because, as with many other relationships, trust can play a big part in our relationship with technology. If we feel we can depend on the product we are using, we have a good foundation for a positive and enduring relationship. If we do not, the relationship may well be problematic, and potentially short-lived.

Establishing trust can take time. Initially, we may be cautious as to how much faith we are prepared to place in an unknown entity and what information we are prepared to share. We may only feel at ease after a number of interactions, connections or encounters. If trust in a relationship can be built up over time, it can also be slowly eroded. A pattern of failure to consider our needs and wishes - a feeling of being let down - can eat away at that trust. Eventually, we may decide that this pattern is so serious that we can no longer rely on a product. This erosion may take days, weeks or months to occur, yet trust can also be destroyed instantaneously. A single major transgression, an infringement of our beliefs and values, can immediately raise serious doubts. Incidents which cause us harm, or which we feel threaten our safety and security, may well bring a relationship to an immediate end.

When we need to establish trust quickly, we might put a product to the test. In preparing for her conversation with Chloe, Kim is concerned about the reliability of the video call technology she is going to use, so she calls Paul beforehand. At first, it seems that her concerns are well founded. The initial attempt to speak to her friend does not go well and Kim's trust in the technology is affected. The second time, however, things improve significantly. There are no guarantees that the call with Chloe will follow the same pattern but the uncertainty in Kim's mind is reduced. She still feels nervous but is better able to keep her attention on the conversation, not the technology which is enabling that conversation to happen.

For the writers at the *Sydney Times*, meanwhile, the editing page which they use to submit their stories presents them with several problems. They do not feel that it is **STABLE**. They have been provided with a tool which could be used as a word processor, but there have been reports of people losing work when changes to articles were not saved.

The journalists have noticed another pattern of behaviour, whereby the page is not always **AVAILABLE** or **REACTIVE** at crucial times. It isn't surprising that this might happen when the system is used most heavily and therefore under greater pressure. For those responsible for such systems, it can help to monitor peaks in usage and to plan accordingly, providing greater system capacity at the times when it is needed. Capacity planning can help to keep systems available when people want to use them, and responsive to their actions and inputs, but this is a complex area where many factors - code, networks, technical infrastructure, even deliberate denial of service attacks - can come into play.

To the correspondents at the *Times*, they probably could not care less about *why* their editing page seems to get stuck. All they know is that it doesn't work when they need it most. The '503' error which Ian refers to occurs when a website is unavailable. It probably means nothing to many of the writers, yet they have seen it often enough that they recognise the code and understand that it means they can't use the site.

This is not a system which they can trust, and their situation shows that sometimes we have little choice but to continue a relationship where trust does not exist. They may not like the page, they may resent its ineffectiveness, and they may discuss their shared misgivings, but it is a part of their working lives and they continue to use it, although they also develop mechanisms for working around the problems they encounter. Perhaps they have similar relationships with some of their colleagues. In a working environment where we might have little choice in who we work with, we might also have little control over the technology we use.

As consumers, we often have more options and more freedom to walk away if the trust in a relationship breaks down. Kim's call with Chloe ultimately went well. The technology did not let them down. But how would she have reacted if the connection had dropped or the sound had been poor, as during the first call with Paul? There is a good chance that her perception of the application she was using would have been significantly diminished. The other factors involved in the call - her tablet, Chloe's computer, the networks they were both using, the servers and other infrastructure - would be of little concern to Kim. This was, after all, a call which really mattered to her. Perhaps she would choose to use a different product in future.

A key factor in our trust in technology is likely to be how **PROTECTED** we feel when using it. When we use technology, we regularly provide information which could be used in ways which might be harmful to us. We may also use devices in different locations, perhaps using unfamiliar networks, or we may take advantage of some of the well-known products which offer cloud storage or hosted applications, which sit on servers in a remote location. Because these technologies rely heavily on elements outside our control, we must place some trust in the organisations which provide them.

Without a good understanding of the kind of vulnerabilities which might leave us exposed to malicious use of the same technologies, we are limited in the steps we can take to protect ourselves. We therefore depend on those organisations to build and provide products in a way which protects us. If we do not feel protected whilst we use those products, we will be unlikely to feel that we can trust them.

Sometimes, serious problems related to our protection can

occur. News stories about technology often relate to data breaches, which might mean that our personal information is no longer **PRIVATE**. Such breaches can affect past customers as well as those who are currently using a product. Failures to keep personal data safe tend to make headlines, sometimes due to the scale of the breach (or, to put it another way, the number of people affected), and at other times because the information involved has the potential to reveal embarrassing or compromising details of someone's life. In either case, when the privacy of our relationship with technology is called into question, the effect on our impression of that technology can be profound, not just for those directly affected but for anyone who hears about the breach.

Whilst breaches may occur outside the boundaries of day-to-day usage of technology, privacy might still be a factor in the impression we form of a product whilst using it. Context is important; particularly the kind of tasks we use the product for, and the nature of the information we are asked to provide. We may, for example, be comfortable with providing an email address to sign up for additional content from a website, but we would perhaps be less obliging if that website requested our passport number, or details from a birth certificate. Meanwhile, an online application for a travel visa would make requests for this information rather more acceptable. Unusual or unreasonable requests would raise questions in many people's minds about how trustworthy a product is.

However, we could not use much of the technology which is so prevalent in modern life without some degree of trust in how our information will be stored and used. Because technology is so intertwined with our lives we can, quite legitimately, be asked to provide a wide range of personal information relating to our personal lives, financial arrangements, health, and much more. This information is held in many places and entrusted to many different organisations.

Consumers have little option but to place some faith in those with access to that data but if that faith proves to be misplaced, the consequences can be serious for both parties.

CLEAR communication can be another critical element in building trust, and a lack of clarity can undermine it. The need to provide customers with an understanding of what data they are being asked for, and why, demonstrates the importance of giving people the information they need, in a language which they understand. Plain language helps to put people at ease, whereas confusing language, or behaviour which prevents us from finding out what we want to know, can suggest that there might be something deceitful happening; there is perhaps something to hide.

This can become apparent (or not, as the case may be) during some of our earliest interactions with some of the websites and subscription services we use, and in the installation of some software. Terms and Conditions - the obligations and legal terms which we agree to when we start using these products - can be confusing for customers, and can lead to misunderstandings. Or at least they might if anyone actually read them.

Kim's reaction to the links to the terms and the privacy policy of the company providing the video call service is not unusual. She is in a hurry, and eager to speak to Paul. She feels uncomfortable but reasons that there is safety in numbers, given the wide usage of the service and the app. Many of us would react in a similar way.

A detailed study[3] by the European Commission in 2016 revealed that between 90% and 95% of consumers will accept Terms and Conditions, yet fewer than 10% will open them if there is an option not to.

Although this demonstrates that people will accept terms

---

[3] The full report can be found online:

http://ec.europa.eu/consumers/consumer_evidence/behavioural_research/docs/terms_and_conditions_final_report_en.pdf without reading them, it does not mean that they feel comfortable doing so, or that they trust the organisation in question. They may simply be resigned to this part of the process. It allows them to move on and do whatever it is that they want to do; perhaps buying something online, installing some software, or registering to use a service.

The same study tells us that providing a simplified version of the Terms and Conditions[4] encourages people to read them and helps create a more favourable impression:

"... simplifying and shortening the T&Cs has beneficial effects... readership is improved, understanding of the T&Cs is better, and the T&Cs are trusted more and perceived more positively... consumers are more satisfied with the content and less frustrated while *reading the T&Cs.*"

If such an approach can help to build trust, the opposite can also be true. When Terms and Conditions are prohibitively long, or difficult to understand, they can give the impression that the organisation providing them does indeed have something to hide. This might not be enough to prevent people accepting the terms, but it may contribute to a negative perception of the product, and the organisation, early in the relationship.

Unless you have a particular fondness for 'fake news' there is a good chance that you would prefer that the information or data you are presented with is not only clear, but also **ACCURATE.** From bank account balances to weather forecasts, from prices of goods and services to data on our health and fitness, we look to applications and websites to provide us with information which we use to make decisions in everyday life. As consumers, if the information we are presented with is inaccurate, this might call into question not just our trust in

---

[4] An excellent example of simpler and shorter Terms and Conditions can be found on the website of the online photography community 500px.com. Their Terms of Service page displays two columns with a full, detailed version of the terms on the left-hand side and a condensed and easy to read summary on the right.

the technology but also in the organisations which provide it.

For Kim, accuracy means carefully researching her story about Australian rugby players moving abroad. She speaks to the player in the late breaking story so that the article she submits is as accurate as possible. This helps to build trust between the readers of the paper, the journalist, and the publication she works for.

In business, accuracy of information is vital. Business information presented in reports about areas such as sales, take-up of services, profit and loss, employee satisfaction and customer satisfaction can profoundly affect the decisions made in those organisations. In both consumer and commercial technology products, the way data and information is calculated, collated, retrieved and presented can affect how accurate it is. Given that providing information can be the primary purpose of many products, accuracy matters.

There is one final aspect we will cover relating to how dependable technology might seem to us (an important element in many successful relationships); how **TOLERANT** of our behaviour it is. A product which makes allowances for the way we behave, even if we sometimes do things which might be a little erratic, is more likely to be one we can depend on.

It isn't unusual for people to feel that they are responsible for something going wrong with the technology they use and sometimes the support, or lack of support, we receive can compound this feeling. The writers at the *Sydney Times* may have experienced this feeling when the IT staff dismissed their problems as 'user error'.

There is an argument that there is in fact no such thing as user error - that any problem which someone encounters with a product can be traced back to the way a product was designed, built, or, crucially, the way in which someone is guided through the process of using it. This might seem like an extreme view, given the many different ways in which people might use a product. However, while it may not be possible to anticipate every problem which might occur, by considering the potential for mistakes the people who create the products may be able to pre-empt them and identify mechanisms to prevent or correct errors, or at least handle them sensitively.

Error messages can be a good example of how products can seem inflexible and unforgiving of human behaviour. They can often suggest that we have done something wrong ('Invalid entry') or that we have been excluded from using some exciting feature ('Unauthorised - Access Denied!'). It isn't surprising that we might sometimes feel that we are being chastised or punished in some way. The use of simple and relevant messages delivered in a friendly, human tone ('Whoops! Looks like we got something wrong') can make a product feel less detached. The use of humour can sometimes bring even more warmth, perhaps sharing a gentle joke at the expense of the technology or the way it works.

If all of this seems like an added burden in the way products are designed, developed and supported; if it seems unfair to ask people working on technology to consider not just technical complexity, but also human complexity - the complexity of the many different people who might use the technology - then there is an answer. You don't have to consider all the people who might use it, just the ones who might occasionally make a mistake.

Here is a reminder of the eight quality aspects covered in this section:

Dependable
accurate available clear private protected reactive stable tolerant

Chapter Seven: Changing times

Dear colleagues,

It is with a mixture of regret and excitement that I can today confirm some significant changes which will affect all of us here at the Sydney Times.

As many of you know, our circulation figures have for some time been in decline. We are not alone in this regard. Our newspaper is feeling the effects of structural changes to the entire news media sector. Many other publications are going through a similar experience.

We pride ourselves on being leaders rather than followers, and on our courage. It is with this in mind that we have decided to bring our publication of a printed weekday newspaper to an end, and to focus our attention on our digital channels and on our printed weekend edition.

This is not a decision which has been taken lightly and I can assure you that the sadness you may feel is shared by me and the board. For almost two centuries, we have been providing the people of Sydney with a daily newspaper and it is natural that some grief will be felt by all of us.

But we must look to the future.

By making these changes now, we believe that we put ourselves at the forefront of a revolution in news media. We can continue to serve the people of our great city, but we can extend our reach and move to a world stage.

Our online presence has been growing, and with it the breadth and depth of the content we provide has also increased. These are trends which we intend to see continuing in the years to come. We aim to position the Times as a global leader in providing rolling news coverage and online content.

Naturally, there will be some uncertainty about what this means for those who work here. Of course there will be some changes in the weeks and months to come. I cannot provide any details at this time but I must emphasise that our intention is not to scale back our operations; rather, it is to grow.

I would like to thank you all for your continued hard work in maintaining the proud traditions of this publication. At the Sydney Times we have always worked to serve our readers by providing them with the news and information they want. We will continue to do so. Let us together move forward into this exciting new era.

With sincere thanks,

John Chisholm

The email from the chairman which was circulated at 9 a.m. that morning confirmed the rumours of the last few weeks. The daily edition of the paper was indeed to be killed off.

Although it wasn't a great surprise to the journalists and other staff, the sense of disappointment and concern in the office was palpable. Kim looked around at her colleagues. Some were quietly discussing the changes which had been announced, while others simply stared at laptop screens, re-reading the email or looking for further information on blogs or forums.

She understood why people might feel worried but she knew that these changes made sense. Clinging to tradition or to an outdated view of what their readers wanted could end up putting them out of business. Advertising revenue from the printed editions was plummeting, according to the reports she had read. People were not buying the paper on weekdays, although the weekend edition was holding up reasonably well. Meanwhile, newspapers from other countries were making their online presence felt and were actively moving into the Australian market. It was right to react.

As these thoughts were running through

her mind, Kim's computer pinged and a notification appeared. Another email, this one from Jonny:

Hi Kim,

You will no doubt have seen the news this morning regarding our weekday editions. Could we please get together this afternoon to discuss some of the changes that are happening?

It might be better to get away from the office, so perhaps we could catch up for coffee. Let me know if there is somewhere convenient for you. How would 3 o'clock suit you?

I'll be postponing our weekly meeting with the team until tomorrow to give everyone some time to absorb today's news.

Regards,
Jonny

Interesting. After involving her in the discussions with AI-Bel, it seemed Jonny also trusted her enough to talk about the changes at the paper. But why not just meet at the offices? She sighed. There was little point in speculating; she would find out what was going on at three o'clock.

She sent a short reply, letting Jonny know that she could meet him later in a café in Pyrmont. The cancellation of the team meeting was a relief as it meant that she could get away from the office and the inevitable gossip which would follow the announcement. Instead, she would be able to focus her attention on the morning's work, which promised to be interesting and somewhat unusual.

Sydney was about to play host to the regional finals of a global tournament and Kim was interviewing a local competitor who had progressed to the latter stages. What made this interview unusual was that the sportsman in question was actually a gamer, a devoted player of a football video game.

Kim had been considering writing an article about the blurring of the boundaries between 'real' sport and virtual sport for some time. The idea had been sparked by a story she had read about a company who used data from a computer game – a football management simulation – to advise clubs in the real world on players they could consider recruiting. The data which supported the game was effectively being used as part of a scouting network.

When she heard about the tournament in Sydney, it seemed a great opportunity to develop the theme. The story had cultural significance, assessing the growth of video games as an influence on society, while the tournament and competitors gave it a local-interest angle. She had woven in some analysis of the *Pokémon Go* phenomenon, which always drew readers, and together these ingredients had made the story an easy sell to Jonny.

Arriving at the venue for the tournament, Kim was greeted by Hugh, the accomplished gamer and interviewee. They made their way into the lobby and found a quiet corner where they could chat. Kim set her trusty digital voice recorder on the table in front of her. She had been using this for years and colleagues sometimes teased her about the aging device. As far as Kim was concerned, it was just fine. She saw no need to change it.

"Hi, Hugh, great to meet you."

"Hi, Kim. Likewise. It's fantastic to be interviewed for the sports pages and I'm pleased to be representing the gaming community."

"Let's start with how you got here."

"Light rail from Central Station," quipped Hugh.

"No," Kim laughed. "The tournament and your place in the regional finals. What did that involve?"

"It's all based on an online league system. I play matches against other people around the world and, based on those results, the players who come out at the top of the league are invited to these finals."

Hugh explained how the competition was divided into groups covering Europe, America, and the rest of the world. Australian players were part of that final group and could be up against players from Africa or Asia in the regional final. The best players from the regional finals would go on to the grand final in New York later in the year.

"There are more places up for grabs in the European and American groups, so in that sense it mirrors real football. The World Cup is heavily weighted towards European and American teams," he added.

"And tell me about the prize money. What's in it for the winner?"

"The top prize is 200,000 US Dollars. Plus the prestige, of course. This is the biggest gaming tournament in the world."

"Serious money," said Kim. "What is it about this game in particular that brings so many players together?"

"Well, I'd put it down to the history of the game and the way it has evolved. A lot of people have been playing for years. There is also a kind of community that has built up around it, with bloggers and support forums and so on."

Kim was keen to get a more personal angle for the story. "What about you? How long have you been playing?"

"From the very start," replied Hugh.

"What people may not know is that this game first appeared back in 1993. I was only ten years old at the time, but I remember Christmas morning that year. I'd been saving up to buy myself a Sega Mega Drive. I hadn't saved enough, but my mum and dad made up the difference, and bought a copy of the game for me too. It was a great surprise. Probably the best Christmas ever for me!"

Kim grinned. This was just the sort of thing she was after. "So, nearly twenty-five years later, you're still playing. What do you put that down to?"

"I guess it's just the way they've updated and improved it each year. Sometimes the changes affect the way you play the game and sometimes they add more depth – being able to play with clubs from different countries, for example. Recently, they added a kind of story mode, where you take a young player through a career in football."

"The game costs around a hundred dollars, doesn't it? Isn't it a little annoying having to pay for a new version each year?"

Hugh replied firmly. "No. Definitely not. I guess some people might find that strange, or think I'm gullible or whatever. To me, I know I will get loads of enjoyment from it, and there are always enough changes to keep me interested, I suppose. Anyway, if I win this tournament that will keep me in games and consoles for the rest of my life!

"I've had a copy of every edition since it was released," he went on. "After the Mega Drive, I moved onto the PlayStation, then PS2, PS3, and now the PS4. The funny thing is, though, that I kept my old Mega Drive – sentimental value, I guess – and every now and then I wheel out the original game and still enjoy playing it. The controls might be different and the graphics might have changed beyond recognition, but the spirit of the game remains. It's just great fun!"

Kim had never been interested in video games but Hugh's passion was infectious. She spent another hour or so talking to him about the community of gamers, the industry, and how he fitted practice and games around his work and family life. She tried her hand at playing on one of the consoles which had been set up in the competition room. It took a while to get the hang of the controls but she felt a great sense of satisfaction when she scored her first goal.

Over lunch, Kim retired to the café in Pyrmont where she would later be meeting Jonny. It was a favourite spot, where she often liked to settle in for an hour or two whilst she caught up on correspondence or worked on writing articles. The staff knew her well and Suzanne, the owner, always made her welcome.

She unpacked her laptop, the voice recorder, some headphones, and her notepad and pen. As she ate her lunch she became engrossed in the story. Andy, the junior writer at work, had once asked her how she could switch into 'work mode' so easily. She had told him that it just came with practice, that she had learned techniques which allowed her to block out distractions and to focus on the task in hand.

So it was today. By the time Jonny arrived, her story was really taking shape. He was happy to hear about the progress she was making.

"This is good stuff, Kim. Only you could make video games seem interesting."

"I don't know about that. It's really popular and it's big business. Hugh was telling me that the games industry is bigger than the film industry. A new *Grand Theft Auto* game release is as big as a new *Star Wars* film."

Jonny shrugged. "Hey, there's a lot of nerds out there." He shifted position in his seat and leaned forward slightly.

Clearly whatever he was going to say next was important. "I know you're probably wondering why I asked to see you today. You might be wondering why we aren't at the office, too."

"Yes, I was a little surprised at that."

"Don't worry. It's nothing serious. I just wanted to discuss something with you privately - off the record, if you like. The shift to a weekend-only paper and a greater focus on our online content is a big thing. The owners want to shake things up a bit and I've been talking to them about a new role for the last few weeks."

"A new role for you?"

"Yes, and some other changes, which I'll explain. This is strictly between us for now, but I wanted to let you know that I'll be taking over as Managing Editor."

"Oh wow, that's big news… I mean, congratulations! But what about Alex?"

Alex was the current Managing Editor and had been with the paper for many years. He was liked and respected by the staff and was seen as a safe pair of hands.

"He'll be leaving us. It's not going to happen right away but the announcement will be made soon enough."

Kim decided it was best not to probe this particular point any further. Jonny had probably been asked to keep the finer details to himself.

"This leaves a vacancy for a Sports Editor," he continued. "I'll be deciding who takes on that role, and I'd like you to apply."

Kim's surprise must have been obvious. Jonny smiled and gave her time to absorb what he was suggesting. Kim composed herself and chose her words carefully. "That's incredibly good of you, Jonny. I'm honoured that you would consider me, but aren't there other people with more experience?"

"Perhaps, and perhaps they might be considered for the role, too. I'm not offering you the position… yet. I'm just saying that I'd like you to be a candidate. You have to understand that things are moving very quickly, not just for our paper but for the industry, and in fact for society as a whole. The technology available to us is changing everything - how we get news and content to people, what content we provide, and when we provide it. We need people who can adapt to that change and in the meeting with AI-Bel you proved that you can do that. You're also a great writer and have an eye for a story. The work you have shown me today is a great example. You're a real asset to us… one of our brightest stars."

He was clearly serious about this. In

Kim's experience, it was very unusual for Jonny to praise people in this way.

"Thank you. Really, I appreciate what you've said. It means a lot."

"Don't tell anyone, will you? I have a reputation to maintain." Jonny grinned. "Oh, and I should also point out that once I start in my new role, I'm probably going to be even more annoying to work with."

"I'll keep that in mind. Are you OK if I have a think about all this? I'm really happy you've thought of me, but I do need to weigh a few things up and if I decide to go for it I have to be certain I really want the job. I don't want to waste anyone's time."

"Sure, take some time - just don't take too much time. We do need to get someone in place. We have big plans for our digital channels, as you know."

The reference to 'digital channels' probably helped explain Alex's departure and Jonny's promotion. Alex was definitely seen as 'old school' by the staff and probably by the owners and publishers, too. He hadn't really embraced the relentless move from the printed page to online content. Jonny was far more comfortable in this new world. Kim's thoughts turned to Ian. How was he seen by Jonny and the hierarchy? She hoped he was not viewed in a similar light to

Alex. Ian joked about the robots taking over but he was not resistant to change. In fact, during their analysis of the uses of the AI-Thor software, he had become increasingly positive, identifying many sports where they could increase their coverage and also recognising ways in which the software could help him personally.

Putting these thoughts aside, Kim said goodbye to Jonny, promising that she wouldn't take too long to let him know her decision. She walked back to the station and made her way home.

That evening, whilst Kim was working on the article, another important email arrived. This one was from Chloe at *Two Halves* magazine.

Dear Kim,

It was wonderful to talk to you last week!
I was very impressed with your ideas during our conversation, particularly with respect to the website, and also with your knowledge of football here in the UK! I have been reading some more of your articles since we spoke and your work is excellent. I am therefore delighted to be able to offer you the role of Deputy Digital Editor for Two Halves magazine. I have attached a detailed description of what the role entails, but let me assure you that there will be plenty of opportunity for you to continue writing and contributing articles for us.

Also attached is a job offer letter which includes details of your salary and other aspects of your employment package. The role will be based at our Manchester offices, but as we discussed there is plenty of scope for travel, both in the UK and abroad. We have included a relocation package in your offer letter, but please do let me know if there is anything else we can do to help in this regard.

If you have any questions at all regarding the role or the offer, please don't hesitate to contact me. I'm really keen to bring you into our team and I will be happy to answer any queries or concerns you may have.

Best wishes,
Chloe Clark

For the second time that day, Kim felt a rush of nervous excitement. As the days had passed since the call with Chloe, she had begun to question whether it had gone as well as she had first thought. It was now clear that her initial reaction was right. She was in demand. It was a great feeling but it also left her with some thinking to do about the job offer from the UK, and the very real possibility of a major promotion at the *Sydney Times*. Kim had a big decision to make.

Durable quality

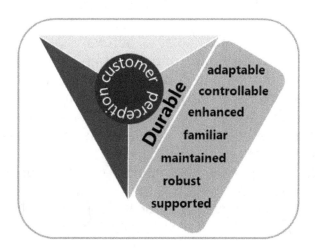

For the purposes of this book and the Three Dimensions of Quality model, the 'durable' dimension relates to how enduring a person's relationship with a product may be, even if their needs and desires change, or the product itself changes. The following section concentrates on seven quality aspects related to durability.

The word 'durable' can also be used to describe something which is able to withstand heavy usage. The distinction between the two meanings has significance for technology because there may be some products which we use heavily, and others which we perhaps use more sporadically. In either case, if the product remains valuable to a person over a prolonged period, the relationship between the two can be viewed as durable.

Kim's voice recorder is an example of a product which falls into the category of heavy usage. She records interviews on the device regularly, and has done so for several years. Because the device is used so heavily, and is subject to physical demands as it is transported between meetings and placed on tables in bars and cafés, it is important that it is **ROBUST**. It must be sturdy enough to cope with this kind of usage.

Robustness is perhaps easier to understand in a physical device - we can visualise the kind of materials and design which might make the voice recorder strong - but it can also be significant in other technology. Software applications, and networks, can be put under strain, mistreated, and deliberately abused. Their ability to withstand this kind of activity can be affected by the way they are designed, built and configured. Whilst this may not be as apparent to the people using technology as the materials in physical devices, the implications of failing to consider robustness may be similar - potential failure in a critical component at a crucial time.

The voice recorder, which is used during the interview with Hugh, has another advantage for Kim. Because she has been using it for so long, it is **FAMILIAR**. Operating the device is second nature to Kim. Its features, which may be limited compared to newer devices, are well understood by her; she has no intention of replacing it yet. There might be more technically advanced products available, and her colleagues might tease her about it, but she has found that it works for her. She gets what she needs from it, the way she uses it has perhaps not changed significantly, and she is happy with it.

Meanwhile, we see during the interview how much Hugh has enjoyed using the football game over many years. What began as a bit of fun; something which he enjoyed with friends and family, now offers something more. He takes the game more seriously (whilst no doubt still getting enjoyment from it) and hopes to use his skills to earn some income. This brings new possibilities, and a new purpose for Hugh in using the game. For him, the product and his relationship with it have proven to be **ADAPTABLE**.

Of course, the game differs from the voice recorder in an important way. There have been changes to it, different versions with improvements and additional features.

There is an interesting philosophical point which might be debated here - whether the different versions of the game represent a *changed* product, or a *new* product. This is related to a question sometimes referred to as the 'Ship of Theseus': is an object whose component parts have changed essentially the same object?

As the name suggests, the basis for the question (as documented by the Greek writer, Plutarch) was a ship belonging to the mythical hero Theseus. As the wooden craft slowly deteriorated over time, timber was replaced to maintain its integrity. Philosophers debated whether, after these changes, the ship remained Theseus' original ship, or whether it was now a different vessel.

More recently, the question was used as the basis for a scene in the UK sitcom, *Only Fools and Horses*. One of the show's characters, Trigger - a road sweeper by trade - is to receive an award from his employer, the local council, who are commending him for saving money. This prudence with public funds is evident from Trigger's care in looking after his broom. Trigger proudly explains that he has maintained the broom for twenty years, replacing its head seventeen times and the handle fourteen times.

Returning to our story, and regardless of the debate about Theseus' ship (or Trigger's broom), what we know is that Hugh has enjoyed the video game over many years and in its many versions. During that time, its primary purpose - to provide a simulation of football which can be enjoyed on games consoles - has remained broadly the same, albeit with substantial advances in how it achieves its goals (if you will excuse the pun).

This is a significant point when we consider the durability of technology. In the case of many products, regardless of changes which they undergo and improvements which might be made, people will often use them for broadly the same purpose as they did at the outset. The purpose can be durable even if the product itself undergoes change.

An example of a product which has proven durable, which many people have used over decades, is Microsoft's spreadsheet application, Excel. It was launched in 1985, initially for Macintosh computers, and then for Windows machines. It has been revised and updated in numerous versions over the years, with new features added each time. Yet its purpose, for many people who use it, remains essentially the same: to store and manipulate data, and to carry out arithmetic functions.

The additional features which have been developed may be of great significance to some who use Excel, but for others they might have little value. The application has survived and thrived over a long period (even withstanding the dark years of Microsoft's animated paper clip) and, along with other Microsoft products such as Word, could stake a claim as perhaps the most successful piece of software the world has seen. Two of the reasons that it has proven durable are that it is adaptable: providing new features and operating effectively on different devices and operating systems, and familiar: successfully fulfilling a basic purpose which has not changed since it was launched.

Two further factors which can contribute to the success of durable products are how well **SUPPORTED** and **MAINTAINED** they are.

Nobody has yet built a perfect product. When our perspectives on what matters differ there is no such thing as perfection and, despite what some might aspire to, in my opinion there is no such thing as 'zero defects'.

This means that at some point, for any given product, a person using it is going to run into difficulties. They may not understand something, or they may find that something does not work for them in the way they want it to. Sometimes these problems might happen for several people using a product, or they might affect everybody using it. This is the nature of technology.

Accepting that this will happen does not mean that those who develop technology do not strive to provide people with excellent products. Neither does it mean that when things go wrong we should despair, and declare those products to have fallen short in the quest for quality. Quality does not mean that everyone who uses a product is always entirely satisfied.

In fact, the response when things don't quite work out can be as important in the impression we form of a product and an organisation as any other factor. For a customer, feeling that we have somewhere to turn when things go wrong can be crucial.

This might be achieved through informative and reliable help mechanisms. Appropriate messages which acknowledge when something has gone wrong and suggest some steps to take can be useful, as can visible sources of help which lead to accurate and relevant information about a product. Moderated forums and online groups, such as the ones Hugh mentions as part of the gaming community, can provide a valuable service in this regard. This kind of dynamic and detailed support can be far more effective for customers, and less costly to run for the organisations which provide products.

Feeling supported might require more than can be provided through help text and forums. Sometimes customers prefer to have someone to talk to, particularly when reporting problems. This can be a costly service for organisations to provide but customers often need to feel that they have been heard.

Beyond this, it can also be important to see that steps have been taken once problems have been reported. Fixing a fault or changing something unpopular might repair, or even enhance, an attentive company's reputation, even if a product wasn't initially everything that customers had hoped it might be.

The visible maintenance of products can help to address specific concerns for people who have noticed those problems, but also demonstrates to others that that there is life in the product. Evidence of improvements, such as release notes provided with new versions of mobile apps, can help to keep people informed, but also shows that there is somebody out there working to improve it.

A point to note here is that product changes are not limited to new lines of code. The sources of help and support might well require maintenance, too. Associated documentation - for example, help text or technical support documents - may need to be adjusted to reflect changes. In a business environment, staff who use a system might also need to be made aware of any known problems associated with the changes, and any workarounds put in place. Overlooking these important tasks could affect the way the product is supported.

Of course, changes and new versions of products do not solely address reported problems. It may be equally important in some cases that a product is **ENHANCED**. This is certainly the case for Hugh, as he explains to Kim during their interview. Each new version of the football game brings with it new features, changes to the game's controls, and more depth.

In some cases, proactive changes can help. Technology companies which monitor the way their systems are used, when they are used, and how heavily, can make adjustments. Sometimes, for example when increasing system capacity to cope with greater demand, customers may not notice the changes. Other alterations, such as making a well-used feature or content more prominent, may be far more obvious.

In Chapter Four, we briefly touched on the subject of Continuous Deployment; an approach which allows organisations to quickly (and frequently) provide updates to products. Changes can be made many times a day in some cases. This capability means that both fixes and enhancements can be made available to customers rapidly. There is a popular view amongst many involved in software development that rapid, frequent change is a positive thing. In the case of fixes to serious problems, there are clear benefits to having a means of quick resolution, but what do frequent changes mean for customers and their perception of a product?

For the early adopters who value novelty (see the Desirable Quality section in Chapter Five), early access to new features may be very important. Rather than waiting weeks or months for something new, they may want updates more frequently. They may want to be among the first to try something and, in return, they may be more tolerant of problems with new features, and may also be willing to provide feedback on those features.

In some cases, where a product has direct competition and where comparisons can easily be made, rapid updates might help in retaining customers who may be tempted to switch to a rival. The mechanisms and practices associated with Continuous Deployment might help a company respond quickly to a competitor's product with a comparable application or feature, or perhaps something even more ingenious.

Yet, it is important to note that change might not always be seen positively in the eyes of a customer. Some people do not want to be early adopters, and some might be very happy with their product just the way it is.

In the case of customers who are perhaps less enthusiastic about changes to things they use, a product which is regularly updated might create a negative impression. Whilst they may be entirely unaware of the concept of Continuous Deployment, they will notice if changes disrupt their ability to do whatever it is they use the product for.

Changes to the 'look and feel' - the recognisable visual elements of an interface - may mean that the product's appearance seems less familiar. Meanwhile, if its behaviour is altered, even in relatively minor ways, established processes can become confusing to people who are accustomed to doing things a certain way.

The mechanisms by which change is delivered can also be disruptive. If deployments require downloads and installations, the time these take can affect a customer's overall perception of a product, particularly if they are in a hurry to complete a task. Constant reminders that there is an upgrade available could cause further frustration: these can sometimes be designed to interrupt the actions which someone is taking, requiring some sort of response before it is possible to return to the task in hand.

The very idea of a change being 'pushed' to a product, rather than 'pulled' by a customer alters the relationship between that customer and the organisation providing the product. The need for control can be a powerful human urge and a feeling of losing control can be uncomfortable. When products are altered without giving customers a choice as to whether, or when, they upgrade, they become less **CONTROLLABLE**.

This raises a more general point about the idea of what constitutes a 'product'. Traditionally, a product had a defined set of features. Customers knew what the features were and made an informed decision as to whether the price of the product justified that feature set. We see an example of this when Kim asks Hugh whether he feels aggrieved at having to pay for a new version of the game each year. Hugh makes a decision to buy the updated product annually, and he clearly feels that this represents value for him.

Under the model of Continuous Deployment, this traditional idea of a product is challenged; a customer may purchase one set of features but find that before long they have a different set. This brings great advantages for those customers who want the benefits of new features and enhancements as they become available. For others, there may be disadvantages. Features which some customers like could be removed or altered without their consent and some may feel that this deprives them of something which they have paid for. Meanwhile, they may be unenthusiastic towards some of the new features. For some, the idea of a changing product might be a turn-off.

As with so many aspects of quality, this is a complex area. Whilst the idea of frequently changing products might be exciting to some, others may be more comfortable to purchase a more static product which will serve them until they choose to make a change. There is perhaps a balance to be struck between enhancement and familiarity, and between updating a product and maintaining its purpose.

The following image is a reminder of the seven different aspects covered relating to durable quality:

Durable
adaptable controllable enhanced familiar maintained robust supportable

Chapter Eight: Moving on

Kim made her way cautiously down the uneven steps, holding on to the sturdy iron railing as she went. Although she was wearing sensible shoes, the stone surface was slippery underfoot after the rain shower which had just passed. The last thing she needed was to fall and make a mess of the smart outfit she'd chosen for her meeting.

She reached the bottom of the steps and checked that the narrow road was clear of traffic then she crossed to the small tarmac area she had spotted from the bridge above. Looking around, she wondered what she had been thinking in coming down here. It was dark, damp, and there was a questionable smell emanating from the large bins nearby. Not a pleasant environment but, as she had suspected, the photo opportunity was much better from down here.

Taking her phone out again, she pointed the camera at the wall above, where there was a painting which depicted a window with a naked man hanging by his fingertips from the ledge. Standing at the window, a man in a suit was unaware of the proximity of the naked man and was peering into the distance in the opposite direction. Next to him, a nervous looking, partially-dressed woman was clearly concerned that her partner (man in suit) was about to uncover evidence of an affair with her lover (man in birthday suit).

Kim chuckled again. She had seen photos of the painting on the internet but not taken from this angle. It added to the comic effect. Making her way back up the slippery steps, she stepped out again into the sunshine, marvelling at the changeable nature of the weather. She took out her phone, opened the messaging app, and found her latest chat with Ian. He was a fan of Banksy, the artist responsible for the painting, and had tipped her off about its location when he heard she was heading this way. She selected two photos of the painting to send to him and added a short message underneath:

Found it! You were right… it's pretty funny

After the message was sent, she opened the maps application to double-check the location of the interview. The hotel was just a couple of minutes' walk from here, over the other side of the green and next to the Cathedral. A few doors away in the opposite direction, she spotted an inviting café with a few small tables positioned out on the pavement. It had been an early start and she could do with a coffee. There was plenty of time. She made her way up to the café and took a seat inside – the outdoor seats were still wet from the rain – then removed her tablet from her bag and set it up on the keyboard stand.

Kim had arrived in Bristol that morning, taking the 7.00am train from Manchester

Piccadilly and arriving in plenty of time for her meeting with Nigel Taylor, the manager of Bristol Rovers. She was working on an article about local rivalries in English football, particularly in the Championship division. In that league, the new season would see derby matches in London, Birmingham, Sheffield, and here in Bristol, where Rovers and City were scheduled to play in a few weeks' time. This article was her main feature for the next edition of *Two Halves*.

It was almost six months since Kim had taken the decision to join the magazine. After deliberating over her options at the *Sydney Times* and *Two Halves,* she had concluded that the move to the UK represented the better opportunity. Jonny had been disappointed that she hadn't applied for the Sports Editor role but he had been pleasantly surprised when Ian had put himself forward and shown great awareness of, and enthusiasm for, their new ways of working. In the end, appointing Ian was an easy decision.

Chloe had been as good as her word and given Kim plenty of freedom to write whilst she worked alongside Grant, learning more about editing and digital media. It wasn't a one-way street; Kim had brought new ideas and ways of working

which Grant had been open to. He had
recently been on a trip with Chloe to look
into establishing a presence for the
magazine in Los Angeles – a base from
which to expand their coverage of the
sport in the USA and Central and South
America. Whilst they were away, Kim had
taken responsibility for all the content
on the website. Things had gone well. It
was clear that Grant had his eye on a role
in LA, so there was every chance that Kim
could be stepping up into the Digital
Editor position on a permanent basis
before long.

For now, her attention was on the day's
interview and the football rivalries
article. As she cast her eye over the work
so far, a tone sounded on her phone. It
was a reply from Ian:

Glad you found it! Got time for a chat?

There was still over half an hour before
the meeting; plenty of time to call her
friend. "Hey Ian, how are you?"

"Pretty good! It's great to speak to
you. Thanks for calling. You liked the
Banksy painting, then?"

"Yes, very good," she said, smiling at
Ian's enthusiasm. "The taxi driver who
brought me over here from the station said
there are a few more paintings around the
city. I'll see if I can spot any others

whilst I'm here. Anyway, how are things going with the job? Is it working out OK?"

"So far, so good. Jonny has been pretty busy so tends to leave me to it most of the time. He was asking after you the other day."

"Tell him I'm doing well, and give him my regards," replied Kim. "How are you getting on with the AI-Bel software?"

"It's gone well, really," said Ian. "We had a few teething problems with some of the early attempts but we're using it quite widely now. Mostly for coverage of local leagues and some of the more niche sports. The good news is there's no sign of the robots taking over just yet."

"Good to hear. Remember if they do come for your job you can always come and work with us."

"I'll keep it in mind. And how are you going? Still enjoying the rain in England?"

"Hey, it's not always raining! Actually, we've had a lovely summer, and I'm getting to see some beautiful places."

They continued chatting while she finished her coffee, catching up on gossip from the *Sydney Times* and sharing stories about life in their new jobs. Kim missed her old friend and mentor, but things had worked out well for both of them. If she had stayed in Sydney and gone for the job as Jonny suggested, maybe their friendship would have suffered.

Once she and Ian had wished each other well and said their goodbyes, Kim packed up her things and made the short walk to the hotel. She waited in one of the grand rooms adjoining the lobby, choosing a table in a quiet corner where she would be able to conduct her interview in peace.

Nigel Taylor arrived late for the appointment, apologising to Kim for the delay.

"Training over-ran," he explained. "We're still getting some of the players back to match fitness after the summer break. Don't put that in the article, though!"

"No, no, of course not, and don't worry at all about the time. You've given me a chance to set up." She gestured to the voice recorder set up on the table in front of them – the very same one her colleagues at the *Times* had teased her about. "Are you OK if we start recording now?"

"Sure," replied the manager. "I understand you're interested in the rivalry between Rovers and City?"

"That's right. In particular, I'd like to get a sense of what it means in the build-up to the derby game. Will you and the players do anything differently when you prepare for that match?"

Nigel Taylor turned out to be an excellent choice of interviewee. He offered real insight into his methods of management, how he motivated his players, and the techniques he used to keep a cool, professional and analytical approach when it came to derby matches – this was his first Bristol derby, but he'd managed teams through many similar situations during his career.

As they discussed his managerial philosophy, he mentioned the scouting tool which Kim had come across when researching the article she had written for the *Times* about the crossover between sport and the world of gaming. He saw Kim nodding in recognition.

"You've heard of this before?" he asked.

"I wrote a piece about video games a while back. I came across it then. I found it fascinating, how the boundaries between sport and games were blurring. Did you know there is even a World Cup for virtual football teams?"

"Yeah – a couple of the players were talking about it," replied Nigel. "They can be a vain bunch. They go on to these games and play matches with animated versions of themselves. I mean, that's a bit weird, isn't it? Seeing yourself in a virtual world like that. Anyway, they get quite competitive about it and a few of them play in these online leagues, so they follow the tournaments. Wasn't it an Aussie who won the World Cup?"

"It was," said Kim. "A guy called Hugh. I interviewed him for that same article, actually. Did you know he won 200,000 dollars for that tournament?"

Nigel let out a low whistle. "That's unbelievable! I guess the boundaries really are breaking down. Some of the players in the lower leagues would love that sort of money."

"Maybe that's why they're playing the game themselves," laughed Kim. "It's not vanity driving them, it's money!"

"You could be right, you know. To be honest, with the younger lads I lose track of all their games and gadgets. It seems like everything is technology these days. When I was playing, we relied on the coaches and manager to spot areas we needed to work on in our game. Now we use wearable devices which follow player movements, we have performance monitoring tools that track heart rate, and so on. We even have a smart ball which we can use to study their technique. It's all incredibly useful stuff, but it feels like the way we work has completely changed."

Kim found herself smiling and nodding again. "It's really no different for us journalists. A lot of what we do has changed over the last ten years. We rely on technology more and more. I guess it's just a reflection of society and the way people's lives have changed."

They wrapped up the interview. Kim was pleased; she had some great comments to include in the feature article. She had also enjoyed meeting Nigel, one of the more engaging and affable football managers she had spoken to. As they made their way out of the hotel, they shook hands and Nigel asked if she was heading straight back to Manchester. She looked around, at the groups of people sitting in the sunshine on College Green, at the grand buildings nearby, and up at the blue sky above them. It was a perfect English summer day.

"I might just stay around and take a look at the city for a while first," she told him.

"I don't blame you. Great day for it!"

He turned to walk away, pulling his phone from his pocket and looking at the screen momentarily. He stopped and looked back at Kim. "I was just thinking about what we were saying, you know, about how all the gadgets and so on help us to do our jobs."

Kim looked at him, slightly puzzled.

"It's like you say," he went on. "It's affecting our whole lives, really. It just seems that it might be an interesting subject for you to write about."

"I did do that article," Kim reminded him.

"Yeah, but that was just about sport. I'm thinking more generally. How technology is always there, how it has changed life. Sometime it helps us and sometimes frustrates us – I mean there is some really useful stuff, but sometimes things just don't work the way you want them to. And because it is so much part of our lives, it can really affect us when things go wrong. Do you know what I mean?"

"Well, yeah. But it's not really something we'd talk about in *Two Halves*."

He considered this for a moment. "A book, then! It's obviously something you're interested in. You're a writer. Why not write a story about it?"

Kim's eyes lit up and she started to smile.

"You know what, Nigel? That's not a bad idea."

In conclusion

As we have followed Kim's story, we have seen the extent to which her life has been affected by the technology she uses. Her day-to-day activities are often guided or assisted by the websites, mobile applications, and other products she uses but there have also been significant changes in her working life, resulting, in part at least, from the effect of technology on her profession.

The ubiquitous nature of the devices which people use to access news stories and articles, together with the influence of social media, has changed the way in which newspapers and other publications provide content online. The days when people relied on a printed daily newspaper are far behind us; news and content are provided on a real-time basis. The applications and websites which deliver that content provide creative opportunities for its delivery, business opportunities for generating revenue - including subscription services or paywalls - and targeted advertising. Meanwhile, the mechanisms for writing, editing and publishing content have also adapted, and Artificial Intelligence has begun to influence the way that some content is written, changing the nature of work for some writers, and perhaps threatening the jobs of others.

Kim has adapted well to these changes, embracing some of the new ways of working, making use of the technology available, and taking the opportunity to develop new skills, whilst refining her talent as a writer.

As she discusses the use of technology in football (and inside footballs) with Nigel Taylor, we see how another profession is changing and how people are adapting. The effects of change are felt in many ways, in many different walks of life, and whilst each of us has a choice as to how far we embrace these changes, there may be risks associated with ignoring the opportunities which they present. Just as the owners of the *Sydney Times* and *Two Halves* magazine need to adapt in order to compete with the social media giants, Nigel and his players have to be aware of how technology can help them stay in touch with the methods which other teams might be adopting. In both cases, a competitive advantage could be won or lost based on their readiness to accept change.

Aside from the influence of technology on her career, we have also witnessed some of Kim's feelings and emotional responses to the products she uses in her day-to-day life. We have seen her frustration at the way in which certain products work (or do not work) for her, and her pleasure when she experiences something which makes her life easier, or which entertains her. These are simple human responses which anyone who uses technology is familiar with. At times, Kim barely notices the products she uses - they simply serve a purpose - and sometimes the lack of an emotional response can be a good outcome. The technology fits seamlessly into her life, helping her do whatever she is doing. At other times, her mood is affected by factors unrelated to technology, or perhaps by earlier experiences with different technology. Kim's frame of mind has a bearing on how she perceives the products she uses.

The influence of mood and circumstances is a reminder of the complex nature of quality which we discussed in the first section of the book - the subjective and variable impression each of us forms each time we use a product.

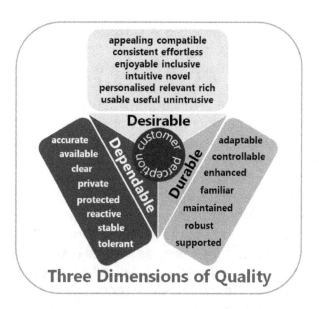

Three Dimensions of Quality

Over the course of the second part of the book, we have looked at some of the aspects which could affect our perception of quality, grouped loosely into the three dimensions: Desirable, Dependable and Durable. We have seen how Kim and her friends, acquaintances and colleagues quickly evaluate the products they use, and how some of these factors contribute to that evaluation. The extent to which they play a part depends on the circumstances under which the products are being used. The significance of the quality aspects and the impression that is formed could be different the next time they use them (assuming that there is a next time). The relationship between person and product is not static.

For those who work in technology development, these observations could be discouraging. If there are so many distinct factors which can affect someone's perception of quality, if what matters varies so much from person to person, and if they are going to change their perception (sometimes as a result of things outside our control), what hope is there? How can we ever satisfy our customers?

To make things even more interesting, the factors which influence a customer's impression of a product cannot be considered in isolation. There are trade-offs to be made. For example, to make a system better protected it may be necessary to add intrusive steps to a process. An application which becomes richer in features may become less responsive as a result. To provide a more personalised experience, there may be a need to gather information which a customer feels compromises their privacy. A product which is regularly enhanced will inevitably lose some of its familiarity, whilst a product which is familiar may no longer appeal to those who value novelty. These are just a few ways in which efforts to address one of the factors may have adverse effects on others.

Despite all this complexity, in the technology itself and the humans who use it, there are, as we have seen, examples of wonderful products enjoyed and valued by millions of people around the globe. There are also techniques and approaches which can be adopted to help in creating such products and some of these have been embraced by the people, teams and organisations who work in this field.

Some of the principles and methods which have emerged in product development are intended to improve collaboration, and to address ineffective and confused communication within those teams and organisations. There have also been improvements in the techniques used to communicate with customers. Interviews, observation, monitoring and other feedback mechanisms can all be effective in bringing the people who develop technology closer to the people who use it. Iterative development approaches present opportunities to refine products, and to improve experiences, based on that feedback.

The key words from chapters Two and Three - empathy and purpose - are common themes in much of what we have discussed. An ability to see the world from the point of view of others, and to understand the kind of tasks or problems they face, makes it easier to conceive of ways to help them. We have seen some examples from other walks of life where this thinking is put into practice, where people are put at the heart of design.

In the development of software and other technology, this same thinking has not always been apparent. There is a phrase sometimes used by people involved in software development which is intended to make a distinction between older ways of working, where quality was sometimes, confusingly, seen as the responsibility of testers (perhaps because it was only discussed once a product had been built and was being tested and fixed), and newer ways of doing things, where techniques are applied throughout development, with the aim of improving quality. It is a phrase which is intended to capture a laudable desire to make quality a shared responsibility for everyone who works in the development of a product. The phrase is 'Build Quality In'.

Yet, this phrase seems to simply shift the burden of responsibility for quality from testers to those who 'build' the product, which inevitably suggests the programmers who write the code. Furthermore, the phrase implies that quality is a tangible and static element of a product; an ingredient which can be added when the time is right. It conjures (in my mind at least) an image of workers on a construction site, stirring water, sand and cement mix together and one of the workers calling out: "Hey, Bob. I'm mixing the concrete - can you bring a sack of quality over here?"

If there is truly a desire to make quality a shared responsibility within product development then it must be a consideration for everybody who is involved in that product's life, from beginning to end. The impression formed of a product, and the experience of using it, is the result of any decision or action taken from the earliest stages of an idea, through experimentation, design and development, deployment, monitoring, feedback analysis, support, maintenance, enhancement, and eventually retirement. Quality cannot simply be tested, or built in. To provide people with something which they value and trust, something which will serve them well over time, we must _think quality in_, not as an ingredient in our product's recipe, but as a consideration throughout the many different tasks and activities which affect it.

For those of us who work in this field, there are incredible opportunities to provide new and exciting products which can have a profound effect on people's lives. If quality matters to us, we need to spend time thinking about it, discussing it with colleagues, asking customers about it, then thinking about it again at every stage. To do so, we need to understand the relationship between person and product, and what affects it. We need to put people, their needs and desires, at the centre of our thinking. If we can do so, we have a better chance of providing quality for humans in changing times.

References and Further Reading

Throughout the book, there are quotes from, and references to, other sources. There are also subjects mentioned which you might wish to explore in more detail.

The following pages contain details of references, as well as suggestions for further reading (not necessarily endorsements). The references are grouped under headings for the chapters or sections which they appear in. The suggestions for further reading are grouped in subject headings.

Quotes and References

Preface

Quality is Dead #2: The Quality Creation Myth by James Bach:
http://www.satisfice.com/blog/archives/251

Premises of Rapid Software Testing, Part 1 by Michael Bolton:
http://www.developsense.com/blog/2012/09/premises-of-rapid-software-testing-part-1/

Rapid Software Testing:
http://www.satisfice.com/info_rst.shtml
http://www.developsense.com/courses.html

Words and Terms

Gerald Weinberg's quote: "Quality Is Value To Some Person" is from *How Software Is Built*:
https://leanpub.com/howsoftwareisbuilt

Chapter One

DJ Derek:

https://en.wikipedia.org/wiki/DJ_Derek

Chapter Two

Jurassic Park:

https://en.wikipedia.org/wiki/Jurassic_Park_(film)

Manifesto for Agile Software Development:

http://agilemanifesto.org/

Chapter Three

The 'Five Room Puzzle':

https://en.wikipedia.org/wiki/Five_room_puzzle

The World at War:

https://en.wikipedia.org/wiki/The_World_at_War

Steve Jobs on Customer Experience at the Worldwide Developer Conference in 1997:

https://www.youtube.com/watch?v=r2O5qKZlI50
(uploaded by 12totu, October 16th 2015)

The theory of 'Six Degrees of Separation':

https://en.wikipedia.org/wiki/Six_degrees_of_separation

Chapter Four

Jon Jenkins' talk on "Velocity Culture" (including a discussion of Amazon's Continuous Deployment capability) at 'Velocity 2011':

https://www.youtube.com/watch?v=dxk8b9rSKOo
(uploaded by O'Reilly, June 20th 2011)

The design firm, IDEO:

https://www.ideo.org/

Chapter Five

Web Accessibility In Mind – an introduction to Web Accessibility:

http://webaim.org/intro/

Nintendo's Wii Fit: http://wiifit.com/

iPhone launch in 2007:

https://www.apple.com/newsroom/2007/01/09Apple-Reinvents-the-Phone-with-iPhone/

Chapter Six

European Commission 'Study on consumers' attitudes towards Terms and Conditions (T&Cs)'

http://ec.europa.eu/consumers/consumer_evidence/behavioural_research/docs/terms_and_conditions_final_report_en.pdf

Terms and Conditions – example of effective use:

https://about.500px.com/terms/

Chapter Seven

Example statistics and information related to people with disabilities or impairments:

Australia
http://www.abs.gov.au/ausstats/abs@.nsf/mf/4430.0

United States
https://www.cdc.gov/ncbddd/disabilityandhealth/infographic-disability-impacts-all.html
https://www.cdc.gov/mmwr/preview/mmwrhtml/mm6429a2.htm

United Kingdom

https://www.gov.uk/government/uploads/system/uploads/at tachment_data/file/321594/disability-prevalence.pdf

Chapter Eight

The 'Ship of Theseus':

https://en.wikipedia.org/wiki/Ship_of_Theseus

Trigger's broom (from *Only Fools and Horses*):

https://www.youtube.com/watch?v=BUl6PooveJE (uploaded by Woody Kane, January 16th 2014)

The history of Microsoft Excel:

http://www.exceltrick.com/others/history-of-excel/ Microsoft's animated paper clip:

https://en.wikipedia.org/wiki/Office_Assistant

The concept of 'Zero Defects':

https://en.wikipedia.org/wiki/Zero_Defects

Conclusion

Naked Man Hanging From Window by Banksy:

https://www.stencilrevolution.com/banksy-art-prints/naked-man-hanging-from-window/

Further Reading

On Quality

The work of Gerald Weinberg:

http://leanpub.com/u/jerryweinberg
http://www.geraldmweinberg.com/Site/Home.html

The work of William Edwards Deming:

https://deming.org/management-system
https://mitpress.mit.edu/books/out-crisis

The work of Philip Crosby:

http://www.philipcrosby.com/25years/read.html

Gojko Adzic on a parallel between software quality and Maslow's hierarchy of needs:
https://gojko.net/2012/05/08/redefining-software-quality/

I also recommend reading *Zen and The Art of Motorcycle Maintenance* by Robert M. Pirsig:

https://www.harpercollins.com/9780060589462/zen-and-the-art-of-motorcycle-maintenance

On Software Development Techniques and Principles

The Agile Alliance website

https://www.agilealliance.org/

The Agile Alliance Glossary of Terms

https://www.agilealliance.org/agile101/agile-glossary/

Martin Fowler's website

https://martinfowler.com/agile.html

The Scrum Alliance website

https://www.scrumalliance.org/why-scrum

Lean Manufacturing

https://en.m.wikipedia.org/wiki/Lean_manufacturing

Lean Startup

http://theleanstartup.com/principles
http://theleanstartup.com/book
https://en.m.wikipedia.org/wiki/Lean_startup

Lean Enterprise

http://en.m.wikipedia.org/wiki/Lean_enterprise
http://shop.oreilly.com/product/0636920030355.do

Minimum Viable Product

https://en.m.wikipedia.org/wiki/Minimum_viable_product

Continuous Deployment

https://www.agilealliance.org/glossary/continuous-deployment/
http://electric-cloud.com/resources/continuous-delivery-101/continuous-deployment/#c9d9-s01-e15 -

Managing the Development of Large Software Systems by Dr. Winston W. Royce. A paper which describes the 'Waterfall model' and its risks:

http://www.cs.umd.edu/class/spring2003/cmsc838p/Process/waterfall.pdf

An explanation of the 'V Model':

https://en.wikipedia.org/wiki/V-Model_(software_development)

On Design Approaches

Urban Design

Responsive Environments: A manual for Designers by Sue McGlynn, Graham Smith, Alan Alcock, Paul Murrain, Ian Bentley

http://www.urbandesign.org/
https://en.wikipedia.org/wiki/Urban_design

Human-Centered Design

What is Human-Centered Design? Explained by IDEO.org:

http://www.designkit.org/human-centered-design

Ted Talk about Human-Centered Design by David Kelley:

https://www.ted.com/talks/david_kelley_on_human_centered_design

The Field Guide to Human-Centered Design:

http://www.designkit.org/resources/1

Seven Principles of Universal Design:

http://universaldesign.ie/What-is-Universal-Design/The-7-Principles/

The Design of Everyday Things by Don Norman:

http://www.basicbooks.com/full-details?isbn=9780465050659

On some of the Quality Aspects

Web Accessibility In Mind – an introduction to Web Accessibility:

http://webaim.org/intro/

Web Accessibility Initiative (WAI):

https://www.w3.org/WAI/

Don't Make Me Think: A Common Sense Approach to Web Usability by Steve Krug:

http://www.peachpit.com/store/dont-make-me-think-a-common-sense-approach-to-web-usability-9780321344755

How the Usability Matrix of Emotions Can Benefit Your Software Testing - an article on the relationship between human emotions and Usability by David Greenlees:

https://www.stickyminds.com/article/how-usability-matrix-emotions-can-benefit-your-software-testing

What Role Do Aesthetics Play In The Design Of A Website? - an article by Steven Bradley:

http://vanseodesign.com/web-design/aesthetics-form-function/

Some examples of visually appealing websites:

https://blog.hubspot.com/marketing/best-website-designs-list

Can you trust technology? – an article by David DeSteno:

http://www.huffingtonpost.com/david-desteno/can-you-trust-technology_b_4683614.html

How is web personalisation affecting the news? – an article by Chris Smith

https://www.theguardian.com/media-network/media-network-blog/2012/sep/04/news-personalisation-content-publisher-media

When New Products Should Make Customers Feel in Control – an article by Ali Faraji-Rad, Shiri Melumad and Gita V. Johar

https://hbr.org/2016/12/when-new-products-should-make-customers-feel-in-control

Miscellaneous subjects

Cognitive bias cheat sheet by Buster Benson featuring the Cognitive Bias codex by John Manoogian III:

https://betterhumans.coach.me/cognitive-bias-cheat-sheet-55a472476b18

List of cognitive biases:

https://en.m.wikipedia.org/wiki/List_of_cognitive_biases

Personas in product development:
https://en.m.wikipedia.org/wiki/Persona_(user_experience)
https://www.smashingmagazine.com/2014/08/a-closer-look-at-personas-part-1/
https://careerfoundry.com/en/blog/ux-design/how-to-define-a-user-persona/

Articles related to the use of automation and AI in journalism:
https://www.wired.com/2017/02/robots-wrote-this-story/
http://mediashift.org/2016/07/upsides-downsides-automated-robot-journalism/
http://www.abc.net.au/news/2015-06-04/dunlop-the-inevitability-of-journalism-written-by-robots/6521560
https://www.theguardian.com/technology/2014/sep/12/artificial-intelligence-data-journalism-media
(This article includes a reference to the automated news story about a Californian earthquake)

Related to female sports journalists, 'trolling' and abuse:
https://www.theguardian.com/media/2016/aug/18/women-sport-rio-olympics-female-sports-journalists
http://www.smh.com.au/nsw/social-media-trolling-of-female-journalists-is-insidious-report-shows-20160305-gnba81.html

http://www.espn.com/espnw/voices/article/15412369/women-sports-media-ignore-abuse

Related to journalism, journalists and their tools:
http://www.currybet.net/cbet_blog/2011/09/csforum11-martin-belam.php
https://www.theguardian.com/info/developer-blog/2014/mar/20/inside-the-guardians-cms-meet-scribe-an-extensible-rich-text-editor

Global football video game tournament:

http://www.fifa.com/interactiveworldcup/index.html

Real world use of a scouting tool from a football management game:
https://www.theguardian.com/technology/2014/aug/12/why-clubs-football-manager-scouting-tool

The use of technology in football training:
https://www.theguardian.com/football/2015/aug/02/science-fine-tuning-elite-footballers

Thanks and Acknowledgements

The existence of this book is testament to the support and influence of many people. Firstly, I must thank my wife, Jules, who has not only been supportive and understanding of the time which I have spent on the book, but has also contributed enormously through discussion, review, suggestions and ideas, along with her knowledge of Urban Design.

I am also indebted to Katharine Smith of Heddon Publishing, for the careful editing, formatting and publishing of the book, and to Catherine Clarke for the wonderful illustrations which bring Kim and the rest of the characters, to life.

Thanks also to Tony Bailey, not only for taking the time to review the text and provide a Foreword, but for the many discussions about quality, specifically Human Quality, which have influenced me and shaped some of the ideas covered in these pages.

Writing *Changing Times* has been a great learning experience for me, not least in researching some of the subjects and examples used. In places, my own research could only take me so far and I needed specialist knowledge and advice on some of the book's themes, so I am extremely grateful to Megan Taylor for helping me to better understand inclusive technology and to Andrew Sonter for making sure that the fictitious world of the *Sydney Times* was not too far removed from the real world of journalism and the newspaper business.

There are many people I must thank for reviewing the book, for discussing some of the ideas as they progressed or simply for chatting about quality and technology. Sometimes even the briefest of conversations have sparked ideas which have grown and developed as I have written the book. Along with Jules, Kath and Tony who I have already mentioned, I am very grateful to David Greenlees, Patrick Prill, James Thomas, Stéphane Colson, Huib Schoots, Carla Medway, Matthew Santon-

Rutherford, Denise Barrett and Greg Barnett. I feel very fortunate to have been able to draw on their collective knowledge and wisdom.

It is important to emphasise that despite all the support, advice and guidance I have received, any errors in the book are mine and not those of the people who have helped me along the way.

There are two other groups of people I would like to acknowledge. Firstly, the experts and specialists who have written and spoken about quality and product development. From books and blog posts, talks and tweets, I have discovered that these are subjects which can prompt wide ranging views, but can also act as pathways to learning about many other subjects. It would be impossible to mention by name everybody who has influenced me, although I have quoted or mentioned some people in the book, and among the references and suggestions for further reading. I would though specifically like to mention Gerald Weinberg, an expert on quality who has contributed so much to the field of software development, and whose writing on the subject shows how it is possible to couple warmth, and a human perspective, with technical knowledge and expertise.

Secondly (and just as importantly), the people who I have worked with over the years; people who I have had many discussions with about ways of working and the quality of the products we have worked on. Without these discussions and everything I have learned from my colleagues past and present, I certainly wouldn't have written this book.

If you have enjoyed this book, we would be very grateful if you would take the time to review it on the Amazon website. A positive review is invaluable and will be greatly appreciated by the author.

Please also visit the Heddon Publishing website to find out about our other titles: www.heddonpublishing.com

Heddon Publishing was established in 2012 and is a publishing house with a difference. We work with independent authors to get their work out into the real world, by-passing the traditional slog through 'slush piles'.

Please contact us by email in the first instance to find out more: enquiries@heddonpublishing.com

Like us on Facebook and receive all our news at: www.facebook.com/heddonpublishing

Join our mailing list by emailing: mailinglist@heddonpublishing.com

Follow us on Twitter: @PublishHeddon

www.ingramcontent.com/pod-product-compliance
Lightning Source LLC
LaVergne TN
LVHW022342060326
832902LV00022B/4199